The Countryside Between the Wars
1918–1940

THE COUNTRYSIDE
Between the Wars
1918-1940

A Photographic Record

Introduction by Sadie Ward
Commentaries by
John Creasey and Sadie Ward

B. T. BATSFORD LTD · LONDON

ISBN 0 7134 1186 4

Printed in Great Britain by
Butler & Tanner Ltd,
Frome, Somerset
for the publishers
B. T. Batsford Ltd
4 Fitzhardinge Street
London W1H 0AH

1 *Half-title page* Poultry, tip-cart
and boatwagon at Aldworth,
Berkshire. Photograph by Eric Guy.

2 *Title page* Ploughman adjusting
the furrow depth of a wheeled
plough. A photograph taken by Eric
Guy at the North-East Hants
Ploughing Match held at East
Worldham near Alton, Hampshire in
October 1938.

3 *Right* Maintenance work on a
water meadow system near
Salisbury, Wiltshire. Channels led
from fast-running chalk streams and
rivers to transfer a thin moving sheet
of water over the surface of the
meadow and to drain it back into the
streams again. The water deposited
nutrients on to the soil and protected
the grass from frost, providing stock
with a rich feed in the early spring
and allowing an abundant hay crop
in the summer. Heavy maintenance
work on the part of the 'drowner'
was necessary to maintain the
correct gradients and allow a
continuous flow of water over the
meadow and to prevent the hatches
and channels from becoming
blocked. In the inter-war years
several thousand acres of water
meadow were still drowned every
winter in the Avon and Wylie valleys
of Wiltshire.

Contents

ACKNOWLEDGEMENTS Most of the photographs in this book have been copied from originals held by the Institute of Agricultural History and Museum of English Rural Life, University of Reading. Where photographs form part of a discrete collection in the Institute, the name of the collection is also given.

General collection, 15, 32, 98, 104, 105, 109, 111, 113, 115, 120, 123, 128, 129, 146, 147, 154, 156, 162

David Brown Tractors Ltd, 45

Council for the Protection of Rural England, 134–6, 163, 164

Farmer and Stock-Breeder, 3, 7, 8, 18, 20, 22, 23, 26, 27, 29–31, 33–5, 37, 39, 44, 46, 47, 49–52, 54, 55, 61, 63, 65, 76–80, 81, 83, 85–8, 95–7, 99–103, 108, 130, 138–43, 152

Farmers' Weekly, 4, 5, 13, 19, 24, 28, 36, 41, 48, 57–60, 64, 82, 84, 90, 91–4, 114, 118, 119, 131–3, 137, 157, 160, 166, 167, 169–76

John Fowler and Co. (Leeds) Ltd, 42

Eric Guy, 1, 2, 9–12, 14, 16, 17, 38, 40, 53, 62, 89, 116, 125, 127, 150, 151, 158, 159

Dorothy Hartley, 144, 148

Noel Long, 122

National Union of Agricultural and Allied Workers, 168

Ransomes, Sims and Jefferies Ltd, 43

John Read, 155

Rural Industries Bureau, 110, 112

Miss M. Wight, 106, 107, 117, 121, 124, 126, 145, 149, 153, 161

The authors and publishers also wish to thank the following organizations and individuals for allowing copies to be made from original photographs or for supplying prints.

Mr E. A. Cory, 66–75

Mr W. Petch, 165

John Topham Picture Library, 21, 25

Mr Ted Smith, 6

The authors also wish to acknowledge the help of their colleagues at the Institute of Agricultural History; they are indebted to Mrs Barbara Holden for her assistance with photographs, to Mr David Phillips for supplying archival reference material and to two successive secretaries, Mrs Phyllis Basten (now with the University's Computer Centre) and Miss Hellen Barnes for typing the manuscript. They are also grateful to Dr E.J.T. Collins for his guidance with regard to the section on farm mechanization in the Introduction and to Mr Bill Petch for his valuable comments on their photographic captions, based on first-hand experience of agricultural practice in the 1930s. The University of Reading Photographic Service was responsible for the expert processing of photographs used in this book. Finally, the Authors wish to express their thanks to Mr Samuel Carr, recently retired from B. T. Batsford Ltd, for his great patience and encouragement in the preparation of this work.

Introduction

The period between the two World Wars was one of crisis for the English countryside. In a climate of acute depression, many came to question the role played by agriculture in national life. Some continued to regard the land as an invaluable economic and social resource; others considered it to be an economic liability and argued that the countryside of the future might be used as a place more for the enjoyment of leisure than for the generation of wealth.

The latter idea would have appeared absurd to economists at the beginning of Victoria's reign; by the end the consequences of the Industrial Revolution for the rural economy were plain for all to see. The rise of manufacturing industry led inexorably to the decline in the importance of agriculture and the traditional rural industries, leaving the countryside progressively denuded of people, their skills and vitality. Britain became a nation of town-dwellers, dependent for food supplies not on her own farmers, but on low-cost producers from overseas, from the Americas, Australasia and parts of Europe. As increasing numbers of steamships unloaded foodstuffs from all five continents at the great ports, for rapid distribution by rail to every part of the United Kingdom, agriculturists bemoaned the ruin of their industry and appealed in vain to successive Governments for protection against foreign competition. But by this time free trade and cheap food were such powerful vote-winners that no party could champion protection and hope to succeed at the polls. By 1914 the contraction of British agriculture had gone so far that only some 30 per cent of the country's food requirements was homegrown; a deficiency that was to have serious repercussions following the outbreak of war with Germany.

During the early years of the war agricultural production continued to stagnate, primarily because the Government offered no incentives to farmers to raise output. By 1917, however, sinkings of British merchant ships by German U-boats were so numerous that a serious food shortage ensued, forcing a change in Government policy. For the first time, farmers' incomes were directly supported by the state; the 1917 Corn Production Act guaranteed prices for wheat, oats and potatoes – a stimulus that resulted in a considerable expansion of the cultivated acreage. By 1918 centralized control had been established over all food supplies – both domestic and imported.

With the return to peacetime conditions, the question arose of whether farmers' incomes should continue to be supported. The discussion hinged on the desirability of further stimulating production. To do so would ensure food supplies in the future, reduce expenditure on imports and create more jobs on the land; some believed that a large self-sufficient agriculture would lead to a more balanced economy with a healthier distribution of population between town and country. Those who disagreed pointed out that subsidizing agriculture would be a costly precedent and might divert funds from industry, the main engine of economic growth. In particular they opposed the suggestion that a policy of subsidizing British agriculture should be accompanied by a policy of insulating it against cheap food imports. Domestic food prices would rise, so too would wages and manufacturing costs, while the agricultural exporting nations were likely to respond to a cut in Britain's food imports by reducing purchases of British exports. The classic argument in favour of free trade remained unanswered – the country's interests were best served by increasing exports rather than by reducing imports. Indeed, there was never any real likelihood that the Government would abandon free trade, and food shipments were resumed in bulk from the early 1920s. Nonetheless, it was decided to continue indefinitely the experiment with guaranteed prices, under the terms of the Agriculture Act of 1920.

For farmers then, the future seemed not unpromising. For landlords it was otherwise. The late-nineteenth-century agricultural depression had already reduced their incomes, forcing the sale of some estates; a trend reinforced by the anti-property legislation of pre-war Liberal administrations. The Great War and the increased liability of estates for death duties (soldier sons often predeceased their fathers) brought more land on to the market. The raising in 1919 of the top rate on death duties to 40 per cent on estates worth over £2,000,000 appeared to owners as a final act of political vandalism, resulting in a further spate of sales. In the four years between 1918 and 1922 some six to eight million acres of England (roughly a quarter of its area) changed hands; arguably the largest and most rapid transfer of land ownership since the Norman Conquest. Thereafter, the flood abated, although intermittent selling occurred throughout the period.

Some land was purchased by the new rich, the urban entrepreneur who wished to acquire a country property for prestige or pleasure. Mostly, however, it was purchased by tenant farmers who bought up their tenancies in the immediate post-war years, encouraged by high prices and Government promises. But in 1921 world prices slumped, the cost of support rose sharply and the Government repealed its Agriculture Act. Farmers found themselves in an unenviable position – burdened with high mortgages and rising costs at a time when incomes seemed certain to fall.

Many reacted by slashing wages. Wages fell on average from around 40 shillings a week in 1920 to 25 shillings a week at the beginning of 1923. An attempt by Norfolk farmers to reduce this amount still further provoked a widespread strike by labourers in that county in the early part of the year. At one point it was estimated that some 10,000 had stopped work; a trial of strength between farmers and workers which, it was widely acknowledged, would decide what happened elsewhere. After bitter negotiations, the labourers won an empty victory: no drop below 25 shillings, but many who went on strike were unable to get their own jobs back, or any employment in farming. The National Union of Agricultural Workers (formed in 1912) learnt a lesson and did not invoke the strike weapon again in this period; the National Farmers Union (formed in 1908), had proved to be the stronger and more effective organization.

The restoration of industrial peace was small consolation to farmers surrounded by steadily growing economic difficulties. In the twenties, Britain became a dumping ground for the world's agricultural surpluses. As the author Michael Tracy points out, wheat-exporting countries raised their output; the invention of chilling made it possible for Argentina to send meat which could compete with all but the best British qualities; New Zealand enormously expanded her trade in meat and dairy produce; Denmark shipped more butter, eggs and bacon; and fruit was sent in increasing quantities from North America.

Little relief was offered by the state. The only concessions were a small subsidy on sugar beet, introduced in the mid-1920s to encourage farmers to risk a comparatively new crop; the establishment of an Agricultural Mortgage Corporation, with limited public funds in 1928; and the abolition of agricultural rates in 1929, although the latter benefited landowners more than farmers.

The stagnation of the twenties gave way to the peril of the early thirties. The collapse of the US stock market led to a world-wide economic recession and to an even more drastic fall in commodity prices; by 1931 world wheat prices stood at half their 1929 level. Most European countries reacted by intensifying existing protectionist legislation, and as these markets were sealed off, the volume of food flowing into Britain increased still further, being a third above normal by the beginning of 1932. To farmers' protests were added those from other sectors of the economy, now suffering from falling exports, increasing unemployment and a collapse of consumer purchasing power. The new National Government, faced with a desperate situation, pledged desperate measures – a comprehensive system of protection. What emerged was a policy of Imperial preference; Empire goods – most of them agricultural – were exempt from paying duty. Britain, it appeared, could not alienate her Empire, even to save her farmers. A strong Conservative cabinet did not find it any easier than its left-wing predecessors to abandon a cheap food policy, particularly during a depression.

Nonetheless, agricultural distress was such by 1932 that the Government was impelled to act. This action took the form, principally, of a return to the subsidies so successfully pioneered during the First World War, supplemented by the creation of Marketing Boards to promote more efficient marketing, and a number of trade agreements with the overseas exporting countries. State intervention, however, was introduced on a piecemeal basis and did not represent a strategy for

British agriculture, or long term commitment to the prosperity of the industry. At best, legislation offered only limited assistance to farmers, and helped sustain incomes until a general economic recovery in world trade was effected in the mid-1930s. The real significance of the 1930s legislation is that it provided the mechanisms for permanent state control, adopted during the Second World War and later incorporated in the 1947 Agriculture Act.

The main change in the agrarian landscape during the inter-war period was a marked decline in the arable acreage of Great Britain which fell from its wartime peak of some 15.7 million, to 11.8 million acres. Wheat, coarse grains and fodder roots were all affected, although the wheat acreage had largely recovered by 1939, a consequence of the Wheat Act of 1932. The twenties saw a recovery of livestock farming as farms were restocked after the war or were grassed down as cereal growing became unprofitable. In particular there was a substantial increase in liquid milk production, a naturally sheltered market, as butter- and cheese-making, severely hit by imports, declined. By the end of the decade the supply of liquid milk exceeded demand, a situation which prompted the setting up of the Milk Marketing Board in 1933 and the promotion of milk as a health food. But the early thirties witnessed a sharp fall in cattle numbers as consumers were no longer able to afford beef and switched to cheaper meats. Rearing tended to be the least profitable enterprise on mixed farms, although small specialist rearers were sometimes worse off; despite cheap imported feeds and later a subsidy and import controls, prices remained low. Arable sheep farmers also did badly, as they could not afford to fold their animals on a succession of fodder crops and only the tougher breeds on run-down hill grazings increased in numbers. The only remarkable increases in production were in fresh fruit and vegetables, immune to foreign competition, and in pigs and poultry – both of which made the transition from 'cottage industry' to intensive 'factory' farming during these decades.

In general, however, British agriculture failed to increase its output over this period. Yields rose slightly – a response to improvements in plant breeding and to a slow growth in the use of artificial fertilizers, but livestock performance remained unimpressive. Much of the beef at this time came from low-quality cows, rather than from specially bred animals; even pedigree herds were produced to conform to established breed requirements, with an eye for the show-ring rather than the market place. In dairy cattle alone was there

4 Women's Land Army, 1918. A training centre for women had been established on Lord Rayleigh's estate in Essex by 1915, and was soon inundated with volunteers anxious to respond to the Government's call for extra labour to help in a 'dig for victory' campaign. Although the WLA numbered some 25,000 by the end of 1917, many farmers opposed having a land girl billeted on them and preferred to take in German or Italian prisoners on the grounds that these could be given heavier or more disagreeable tasks. However, after proving its usefulness, the Land Army was disbanded just before Christmas 1919.

any notable change; average output per cow rose from a pre-war figure of about 550 gallons for each lactation to over 800 by 1939.

Most farmers responded to depression by limiting expenditure. The result was lowered standards of cultivation, bad drainage, overgrown hedgerows and buildings allowed to fall into disrepair. It was a period when, in A. G. Street's words, it was no longer customary 'to do one's duty by the land'; there was little incentive to mechanize or to take risks.

In retrospect, of course, this period saw the growing importance of the tractor and the beginning of the end of horse husbandry. Yet there was no sudden transformation in the power economy of the farm; 'nearly 650,000 horses were still employed (in British agriculture) in 1939, accounting for more than half the total draught power and doing about two thirds of the total work' (Collins, unpublished).

Many early tractors were badly designed, overweight giants built to imitate the steam engine rather than the horse, and generating little effective draught power. Often they came to be used purely as stationary engines for threshing and barn work. The most successful tractors were the American lightweights, notably the Fordson and the International Harvester. The first generation of tractors had a short working life and were plagued by poor starting, poor lubrication and wheel slippage – a problem not completely solved until the introduction of the heavy-duty pneumatic tyre in the early 1930s. Moreover, the conventional tractor could not be used for certain specialized operations such as inter-row cultivation; the American row-crop tractor was eventually to meet this need in the 1930s. Another constraint was the lack of purpose-built implements. Adapted horse implements were awkward to use and single-hitch connections, while sometimes very ingenious, were on the whole unsatisfactory; any unevenness in the ground was liable to throw the implement out of its work, causing delay or even accidents. The three-point-linkage, invented by Ferguson in 1920, was a partial solution but was not widely employed until the development of the hydraulic lift in the mid-1930s.

In general, tractor design and reliability improved greatly during the 1920s. Indeed, farmers were deterred more by considerations of comparative cost than by technical defects. Collins, in unpublished research, has estimated that tractors were economic only in very heavy work, such as ploughing or binding, where they might displace as many as five horses. The chief advantage of tractors was their greater speed, which was especially important on heavy soils and in wet seasons. Even so, tractors were seen more as a adjunct to, than as a substitute for, horse-power until at least the mid-1930s. Before this horses were extremely cheap, due partly to a fall in demand as the arable area declined, but also to the throwing on to the market of large numbers of town draught horses with the advent of the motor-lorry. From about 1920 the size of the horse population diminished progressively, although, to the horse-lover, the more disturbing trend was the decline in horse-breeding to the point where the horse population was failing to reproduce itself and eventually would have become extinct. By the mid-1930s horse deaths had assumed, in Collins' words, 'frightening proportions' (50,000 in 1933–4 alone); thereafter the more restricted supply of young horses caused prices to rise, giving a fresh impetus to the breeding programme, although birth rates were still lower than in 1920 and the decline had only been slowed, not reversed. None the less, horses remained the best buy on small farms, particularly in the pastoral north and west; it was only in the arable east and south that the tractor had become predominant.

Another significant technical advance was the introduction into Britain of the combine harvester. Such machines had long been in use on the extensive corn lands of the American Midwest, but they could not easily cope with the smaller acreages and often awkward field shapes of British farms. Driving a combine was a skilled job; machines had to be driven slowly if they were not to clog on the heavier British crops, as much as two hundredweight of corn per acre could be lost by an inefficient operator. Often it was cheaper and easier to use a horse or tractor-drawn binder and hired thresher, especially as the purchase of a combine ideally entailed additional outlay on drying plant – a major expense at a time when many agricultural merchants refused to take combined and artificially dried grain for seed, and when corn prices remained depressed. Only some 50 combines were reported as having been employed on the 1934 harvest, although this had increased to 940 by the first census of machinery on farms carried out in 1942.

Hand work was still the normal method in many field operations, notably in the planting, singling and lifting of root crops. The design of a machine capable of discriminating between stones and potatoes proved difficult and satisfactory potato and beet harvesters were not developed until after the Second World War. On smaller dairy farms milking was still usually carried out by hand, often in old-fashioned and inconvenient buildings. A experiment, however, in low-cost milking that attracted much attention in Southern England was that of open-field milking on the Hosier principle. In 1920 A. J. Hosier had bought a thousand acres of derelict land on the Wiltshire downs, to which at the end of the 1920s he added another 1500 acres in the adjoining parish. Convinced that the future lay with dairying rather than with corn growing, but without suitable buildings, he decided to keep his cows out of doors all year round. The cows were milked by machine in home-made corrugated huts or bails, moved over the pasture from one paddock to another. This system saved greatly on labour, but was suitable only for light land capable of carrying a herd throughout the winter without churning up the soil.

Hosier was one of a number of entrepreneurs who gradually expanded their businesses, either in acreage or in intensity of operation, at a time when land could be bought or rented very cheaply. Another innovator was P. Webster Cory, who took over Notgrove Farm in Gloucestershire in 1916 and gradually converted the mainly arable enterprise into a 1,000 acre grassland 'ranch'. A number of photographs taken from a family album, illustrating this process in the 1920s and 1930s, are reproduced in this book. From about 1933, however, it is possible to discern a movement towards more intensive forms of production, using cheap imported feeds, more machines and integrated farming systems. Higher costs were repaid in higher output which enabled the progressive farmers to drive their weaker brethren out of business. Clyde Higgs, of Hatton Rock, Stratford on Avon, typified this new approach. Concentrating on dairying, he invested in a range of special machinery – the Wilder 'Cutlift' to mow the grass, a drying plant to artificially dry it, and a purpose-built cow house with the very latest milking machinery. The profitability of each operation was carefully monitored; balanced rations and scrupulous milk-recording turned the dairy into a success, but grass-drying was abandoned when it failed to show a profit. Higgs also put in electricity, although few farmers had the means to purchase transformers to boost lighting plant to the 240 volts necessary to run machinery. Rural electrification, like other forms of modernization, was largely a post-war development.

Agricultural science, too, made only a limited contribution to British farming in this period. Important work was carried out by a number of exceptionally gifted scientists, but research was not quickly translated into practice. Farmers resisted new knowledge where this conflicted with

5 German prisoners-of-war bagging potatoes in Surrey in 1919. Prisoners began to be used in any quantity only in 1918, but by the time of the Armistice over 30,000 were employed, especially in field work like hoeing root crops and lifting potatoes. Many prisoners were already familiar with farm work and they were normally regarded as good labourers by English farmers.

tried and trusted methods, or where the adoption costs were high. In the 1920s, for instance, Imperial Chemical Industries began to demonstrate, at their Jealott's Hill research station in Berkshire, how grass might be improved when supplied with adequate nitrogen, phosphates and lime. But some farmers were discouraged by the additional expense; others found that unless the correct procedures were observed 'nitrogenous fertilizers led to such rank growth in grass that clovers were suppressed and the feeding value of the sward badly damaged; corn crops sown after a fertilized ley were apt to go down before harvest, with extra costs and worry before they could be cut' (Whetham, 1978). Despite the efforts devoted to grassland research in the thirties, standards of management improved only slowly. Surprisingly, perhaps, fruit growers benefited more from scientific advances at this time, as new high-yielding and resistant strains became available to provide another stimulus to an already buoyant industry.

Teaching farmers how to 'practice with science' was not an easy matter. The majority of small family farms were run by men with little schooling and no technical education. Farm advisory services were run by County Councils, and the larger counties had set up farm institutes to provide some practical instruction, supported by scientists and economists at eleven regional centres. But such services remained limited owing to the poverty of Government funding. Indeed, farmers probably learnt more in a general way from the agricultural press; the *Farmer and Stock-Breeder* (dating from the late nineteenth century) and *Farmers' Weekly* (from 1934) commanded a wide readership amongst all sections of the rural community. Articles by scientists, economists and working farmers (such as A. G. Street, whose column in *Farmers' Weekly* combined common sense, shrewdness and a natural wit in equal parts), all helped to make farmers better informed and encouraged them to adopt a more efficient and business-like approach.

Profitable farming, however, was achieved by comparatively few; some of the most as well as some of the least efficient failed, and left the industry. Those who derived part of their income from sources outside agriculture were often better off, being able to subsidize their farming in this way, but those with little capital only survived by dint of hard work, with no time for leisure or relaxation. Some endured and did well enough, to find in the thirties that their sons preferred to pursue a less exacting occupation with greater security and a pension on retirement. Overall, there was a high turnover of personnel; in Dr E. J. T. Collins's evocative phrase, 'whole farming dynasties were wiped out in a single generation'.

Labourers, too, migrated to the towns in large numbers; farmers employed fewer men while urban life held attractions of its own. The agricultural workforce declined by about a third between the wars, as a quarter-of-a-million men left the land. Another contributory factor to rural depopulation was the continued decay of many traditional country occupations; the long term result of industrialization, aggravated by agricultural depression as well as by changes in the consumer demand for food.

Many small country food retailers were bankrupted by the growing preference of British housewives for better-quality, packaged and branded foods, supplied by large wholesalers. This was true, for instance, of the bread trade – small masterbakers were replaced by industrial bakers, and of the milk trade, where the large plant dairies came to dominate the milk market. Urban shoppers preferred the wrapped, sliced loaf, even with the vitamins rolled out, and bottled milk instead of that ladled out of a churn. There was a small growing demand for 'health' foods – for Hovis bread, cereals and fruit-juice; but the food trade was predominantly geared to the requirements of the mass market. The growth of road transport, new techniques of chilling, freezing and canning, and the development of multiple retailing all had the effect of eliminating traditional markets and substituting new national ones. At the same time, British goods frequently sold at a disadvantage compared with overseas products, since they tended to be of varying quality and were unpacked and ungraded, whereas imported goods tended to be packed to suit the requirements of wholesalers and were graded to uniform standards. In order to overcome this deficiency, the Ministry of Agriculture was given power in 1928 to assign quality grades for British agriculture and to licence sellers to use the National Mark on graded commodities. Even so, the quality of home-grown goods lagged behind that of Britain's competitors; despite George Orwell's distaste for the 'shiny, standardized, machine-made look of the American Apple' (*The Road to Wigan Pier*, 1937), buying foreign was often best.

The ready availability of cheap manufactured goods had virtually destroyed the older rural industries in the late nineteenth century. Factory production and foreign competition combined to ruin the underwood trades; the makers of baskets, besoms, barrel-hoops and all manner of coppiceware contrived to meet the intricate demands of a once-diverse rural economy. The larger village manufactories had mostly disappeared, leaving only dwindling numbers of ageing craftsmen, too old to learn new skills and condemned to lead an increasingly solitary and impoverished existence. Even those trades directly servicing agriculture were affected; 'the scythe-handle and the rake-maker did not long survive the mechanization of the hay and corn harvest, nor the hurdle-maker the demise of the arable flock and sheep-fold,'

6 This photograph is remarkable in illustrating all three forms of farm motive power: the ox, the horse and the tractor. It was taken in the 1920s on Earl Bathurst's Cirencester Park Estate, Gloucestershire. Ted Smith, seen at the plough behind the ox team, retired as Britain's last oxman in 1963. The six Hereford oxen are drawing a double furrow plough and the horse team a single furrow plough. The International 10–20 tractor, which was popular in Britain from the early 1920s to the beginning of the Second World War, hauls a multi-furrow trailed plough (see also no. 126).

(Collins). Moreover, the future of the wheelwright, blacksmith, saddle- and harness-maker was secure only as long as the agricultural horse remained the predominant source of draught power on the farm. By the 1930s this supremacy was no longer assured and by then, too, the contraction of the arable acreage had hit small engineering workshops and even the business of the larger implement makers by reducing the demand for cultivating and harvesting equipment. Country brickmakers also found less demand for drainage tiles as underdraining was not maintained, while at the same time factory-made bricks reduced the building supply side of their trade. In many areas depopulation led to a slump in house construction, although some rural builders benefited from the outward expansion of the suburbs in the interwar period. A detailed survey of the rural industries of England and Wales carried out for the Agricultural Economics Research Institute at Oxford between 1919 and 1923, however, painted a gloomy picture of decay. Temporary as well as permanent employment was much diminished; a situation all the more serious because it threatened the survival of the rural jack-of-all-trades, who carried out the many small, but invaluable services – such as carting and hauling, and strictly seasonal work – indispensable to the functioning of the rural economy.

The 'victory' of the urban, industrial state alarmed many intellectuals who refused to accept the view that rural decline was a sign of general progress. They considered, to the contrary, that the withering away of the old self-dependent village communities represented a weakening of the county's moral and economic strength and involved the loss of much of its culture heritage. H. J. Massingham was only one of a number of writers who urged the need for positive measures for the regeneration of rural life, necessary to 'regain our national health and save us from the dreadful regimentation of living, thinking, playing and working which hitherto is the contribution of twentieth-century Europe to the history of the world' (Massingham, 1934).

Concern was expressed even in Government circles; the Ministry of Reconstruction issued a report in 1919, noting:

The whole question of rural industries is prejudiced by the general feeling that they are individually insignificant and represent a sort of survival from an earlier stage of industrial development; that, in short, they are in a fair way to extinction by the larger factories and that any effort to revive them is simply attempting to swim against the stream of economic progress. This is surely a fallacy, ... In changed circumstances, it would seem practicable for many of these factories and shops to be placed in

villages or small towns and thus to provide alternative occupations for the rural community.

Support for a totally 'balanced economy', however, was forthcoming only from extreme political groups; the more reactionary elements in the Tory party, for instance, wished to restore the old English yeomanry, with its instinct for property and patriotism. But if the extolling of peasant virtues struck an answering chord in Nazi agricultural policies a decade later, the British Government's interest was more solely in dealing with the pressing problems of demobilization and rising urban unemployment.

Thus the Rural Industries Board, set up in 1921 under the direction of the Ministry of Agriculture, was an unambitious attempt to keep rural workers on the land and out of the already forming urban dole queues. The Board's aims were limited; to offer practical aid to country craftsmen already in business, principally in those trades servicing agriculture; and to help others get started. Undoubtedly, its work benefited small numbers of individuals, but as an instrument of any wider reconstruction it was hopelessly inadequate. The sharp increase in the numbers of jobless in the early 1930s brought a fresh Government initiative, the attempt to settle the long-term industrial

unemployed on the land. The Land Settlement Association, inaugurated in 1934, purchased farms in different parts of the country and divided these into smallholdings – mainly for vegetable, pig or poultry production. Each tenant became a member of the farm co-operative, which bought supplies, organized marketing and provided a central pool of machinery. Similar schemes were run by some county councils, while the Salvation Army offered agricultural training for the unemployed on its farm colony at Hadleigh in Essex. As it turned out, however, the urban jobless often had no wish to be 'rescued' from the miseries of industrial life; as Whetham (1978) comments, 'nearly half the men transferred by the Land Settlement Association to other districts returned home within eighteen months, preferring unemployment to the strangeness of rural life in Cambridgeshire, Bedfordshire, Suffolk and Gloucestershire'. The other schemes enjoyed no greater success.

This antipathy to the countryside was not shared by all townspeople. A growing number of

7 Shorthorn cows making their way through a muddy gateway in the Stowmarket area, Suffolk, 1934. This is an example of neglected and mis-managed grassland. Underdrainage is required and winter grazing needs to be reduced.

middle-class families saw rural England as an attractive habitat, where they could escape from the shabbiness, noise and dirt of the industrial cities. Something of this sentiment was caught by George Orwell in *Coming up for Air* (1939) in which he was preoccupied with a vision of the old, unspoiled countryside before the Great War – a place of human retreat and quietude. But, ironically, when George Bowling (the central character in the book) returns to the Oxfordshire village of his childhood after an absence of over 20 years he finds instead a middling-sized town – with brand new estates of red-brick houses, inhabited by migrants from London and Lancashire. Similarly the poet, Edmund Blunden, deplored the appearance of the stockbroker belt and the more expensive 'marzipan misconstructions' which 'insulted the Sussex Downs', while Clough Williams-Ellis wrote scathingly of the whole process of suburban colonization in *The Face of the Land*, published in 1930:

> Further and further afield the adventurous bungalow plants its frail foundations – a pink asbestos roof screaming its challenge across a whole parish from some pleasant upland that it has lightheartedly defaced. It is thus, through ignorance and not through malice, that we are losing our inheritance of beauty. Day by day, year by year, tree by tree, acre by acre, the old England perishes away.

The 'desecration' of the countryside was, in Williams-Ellis' view, the result of the invention of the internal combustion engine:

> Came the motor 'bus, the motor bicycle, the little car, and with them 'ribbon building' along the roads, the squalid establishments to serve the machines and their passengers and the touting announcements to catch their insensitive eyes.

The proliferation of advertisement hoardings, unsightly tea-shacks and petrol depots along Britain's rapidly developing arterial road network provided the background for one of the earliest conservation movements. In 1928 the Ministry of Transport encouraged the setting up of the Roads Beautifying Association, with the object of improving highway appearance through plantings of trees and shrubs and the laying out of grass verges. Such action, however, did not touch the core of the problem – the need for effective planning controls over virtually unrestricted urban growth in rural areas; this campaign was undertaken by the Council for the Preservation of Rural England after its formation in 1926. One important contribution made by the CPRE in its early years was the support which it gave to the movement for National Parks and the provision of public land for amenity and recreational purposes. The idea that land of outstanding natural beauty should be preserved for the nation had been pioneered by the National Trust, established in 1895, but by the 1930s the Trust acted more as a landholding than a propagandist organization – concentrating on the acquisition of country houses and small estates. The CPRE was chiefly responsible for the appointment of a Government Committee which reported in 1931 in favour of a series of national parks, to be paid for out of public funds. Nothing, however, was achieved until after the Second World War.

The desire to improve access to the countryside dated from the late nineteenth century. At first, much of the impetus came from middleclass intellectuals who encouraged urban slumdwellers to make more fruitful use of their leisure hours by taking part in some outdoor activity organized on their behalf. But before long the working classes responded by forming cycling, rambling, camping, field and camera clubs of their own. Both types of organization tended to be influenced by the ideals of John Ruskin and William Morris; participants hoped, through the enjoyment of nature, to develop a sense of fellowship which anticipated the collectivity of a socialist society. But by the 1930s such high-mindedness was less in evidence, as thousands of men and women took up hiking or camping as a cheap form of recreation. During the Depression years, countless numbers fled the factory towns of the Midlands and North to spend their Sundays walking the moors and fells. By 1931 the Federation of Rambling Clubs had over 40,000 members, a figure which did not include individual hikers. Yet rambling activities were still restricted by lack of access to open spaces, especially in the north Pennines where the grouse moors were regularly closed to walkers – an occurrence which often led to conflict between ramblers and landowners. To put pressure on the Government to open tracts of land to the public, ramblers held annual rallies at Winnats Pass near Castleton in Derbyshire, resulting, on at least one occasion in 1932, in clashes with the police and a number of arrests. An Access to Mountains Bill was finally passed in 1939, but it was an inadequate measure which never came into operation, and the opening up of many areas had to wait until the National Parks and Access to Countryside Act of 1949.

The need for inexpensive holiday accommodation for young people was met by organizations such as the Cooperative Holiday Association

(1891), the Holiday Fellowship (1913) and later by the Youth Hostels Association. The former organizations were founded by T. Arthur Leonard, a Congregationalist Minister, who afterwards became the first Vice-President of the YHA in Britain. Youth hostelling was first developed in Germany before the Great War, and spread rapidly through France and Holland in the 1920s; a National Association was established in Britain in 1930. The popularity of hostelling owed much to the sense of adventure and internationalism which it promoted, although in Hitler's Germany the youth movement was to be subverted into serving more chauvinistic purposes.

For those with more money at their disposal, holidaying in rural England could be enjoyed in leisurely fashion. Horse-caravanning was in decline by the 1920s, but the next decade saw the growth of motor-caravanning, aided by improvements in car manufacture and the use of new light strong materials in the trailer itself. Motor-caravanning was promoted by the motoring organizations and journals; *Autocar* staged a rally at Minehead in 1932, the Junior Car Club another at Brighton the same year, and the Royal Automobile Club yet another at Cheltenham in 1933. The Camping Club (1906) also formed a caravan section at this time, while the Caravan Club was refounded in 1935; another milestone was the appearance of the world's first caravan paper, *Caravan and Trailer*, which provided much useful information. Indeed, all the open-air societies seem to have bombarded their members with maps, guides and monthly or quarterly magazines, detailing the best equipment, routes, sites and tourist accommodation. For those who preferred to do their own planning, journals such as *Open Air*, which ran briefly in the early twenties, suggested areas where more intrepid holidaymakers might 'get away from it all'.

The impact of this urban invasion on the rural community was greatest in those villages within easy travelling distance of London and the larger cities, along the south coast, and in the developing holiday regions. It was least in those areas remote from the centres of population, particularly in the north and west, and in parts of East Anglia. Where small farms and smallholdings predominated and the struggle to survive was hardest, a common poverty often drew the community more tightly together and made it more secretive and resistant to change. Here, if anywhere, ancient custom and primitive belief lingered for a while, and the educated talk and habits of townspeople were scorned. Curiously, the large arable parishes of Southern England were often less democratic; the squire and parson still predominated in local government and took pride in presiding over the work of innumerable committees. The old paternalism had been outgrown by the coming of the welfare state, but the church hall remained the venue for a wide range of improving activities, and the village cricket team rarely consisted of the best eleven available, regular players being dropped to make room for visiting gentry. Fox-hunting, too, remained the preserve of the better off; the labouring classes could only follow the hounds on foot or on bicycle.

Village life, however, was not immune to the spread of urban culture. Most traditional games and pastimes had already disappeared, unless reintroduced by the local schoolmaster or emigré intellectual. Thus the poet, Robert Graves, and other ex-soldiers restored the game of football to Islip in Oxfordshire after a lapse of some 80 years – although the village nonagenarian complained that the game was not now so manly as in his boyhood.

> He pointed across the fields to a couple of aged willow trees: 'Them used to be our home goals', he said. 'T'other pair stood half a mile upstream. Constable stopped our play in the end. Three men were killed in the last game – one kicked to death; t'other two drowned each other in a scrimmage. Her was a grand game.'
> (*Goodbye to All That*, 1957 edn)

In many ways change was indisputably for the better. Wages and conditions of work varied in different parts of the country, but there was a slow, general improvement from the mid-thirties. Greater mobility was also achieved. With the development of bus services, country dwellers could enjoy more frequent and comfortable travel to nearby market towns; some among the younger generation might make regular visits to the picture house, bringing them into contact with the glamour and romance of Hollywood. Even in the most traditional village pub the talk was more of football pools and less of purely parochial matters; a darts match might be broadcast nationwide over the wireless and there were few country people by the end of the thirties who did not have access to this latest invention of modern science.

Rural children, too, benefited from a better education than their parents. The provision of schools and quality of teaching was usually worse in rural areas than in the towns, but more children stayed longer at secondary school, and some of the brightest went on to University or Teachers Training College. The Workers Educational Association offered a second chance to adults who had left

8 A Gyrotiller clearing derelict land on the farm of C. E. Best, Fifield Bavant, near Salisbury, April 1937. Mr Best was clearing 50 acres out of some 200 acres of waste land lying at 500 feet on his 1,000-acre farm. The cost of tearing up the gorse, hawthorn and trees, some 10 feet high, was about £5 per acre. Following the burning of the rubbish and further ground clearance the land was to be put into arable cultivation to see if an adequate wheat crop could be grown on it. The Gyrotiller, a tracklaying machine fitted with power driven rotary cultivators, was developed by Fowler of Leeds from 1927 to pulverize the soil of Cuban sugar fields without drying it out. About forty of the 170 hp diesel-engined machines were produced for the home market in the early 1930s and most of them were employed by contractors, like this example owned by Oxfordshire Land Cultivators. Problems in running Gyrotillers and the manufacturer's failure to improve the design and market it adequately, led to their withdrawal from service within a few years.

school at an early age. In some areas, it is true, the WEA soon lost its working-class following and became largely middle-class in its composition, but Fred Kitchen noted with gratitude in his autobiography, *Brother to the Ox*, that, after enrolling in 1933, he was able to study literature, music, psychology and economics, and moreover was encouraged to write.

There was little improvement, however, in cottage accommodation. Families continued to live in two-, three- or four-roomed cottages which were low-ceilinged, dark and damp. The tied-cottage system, whereby if a man lost his job he lost his home too, was greatly resented by agricultural workers. Some county councils were active in buying up and reconditioning old cottages or in building council houses, but it was estimated in 1939 that some 250,000 homes were still needed to house adequately people employed on the land.

Many labourers' wives continued to use candles or paraffin pressure lamps for lighting, to carry water in heavy buckets from the well, and to cook on a coal fire with the oven on one side and the hot water on the other. Yet piped water and electricity were slowly reaching rural areas, and council houses, even if ugly and ill-appointed in other respects, generally contained more accommodation and were better provided with amenities than most cottages. The best were well designed and possessed adequate land for the labourer to grow vegetables and even to keep a pig at the back. Rural council homes also retained their proximity to the village shops and pub – the heart of the local community – unlike the worst estates on the edges of the industrial cities. Even so, it was in the farmhouse, parsonage and other middle-class homes that the new labour-saving devices were mostly to be found – a kitchen range supplemented by an oil cooker, a hot water system which supplied the scullery and bath, and an inside flush toilet, requiring a septic tank costly to install.

But increased contact between town and country taught village people that primitive conditions and a life of unrelieved drudgery did not have to be endured. Whetham comments: 'Fetching water from the well or standpipe, scrubbing the children in a tin bath in front of the fire, and emptying it afterwards into the garden, the outdoor earth closet, were recognized to be old-fashioned habits dictated by poverty and by the absence of public facilities which the urban families took for granted.' In consequence, many rural families left for the towns; some to find that urban squalor could be even more depressing and hopeless, others to find more highly paid employment and better prospects. Those who stayed were, in time, able to demand and achieve a higher standard of living, not through charity, but through hard bargaining and increased state provision.

The dynamic nature of rural life, however, often escaped the attention of townspeople, many of whom retained an idealized perception of the countryside, despite their greater acquaintance with it. Journals such as *The Field* and *Country Life* – with their articles on country house living, fox-hunting, shooting and Ascot, on archaeological curiosities, old recipes and rustic sayings – gave substance to an image of the countryside essentially serene and unchanging. Yet beneath this surface tranquillity, even upper-class society was in turmoil, as many landed estates changed hands or their owners were forced to adopt a more frugal lifestyle. For farmers, as we have seen, the effects of depression could be equally demoralizing; the struggle for survival, as chronicled in the pages of the farming press, was frequently brutal. One result was the emergence of a more pastoral, less husbanded landscape, in which England's green and unprofitable farmland assumed an unkempt and even derelict appearance. It was an age which witnessed, in A. G. Street's memorable words, the 'waning of the farmers' glory'. But at the same time, the face of rural England was also being transformed by the 'octopus' of urban growth, which in itself posed new challenges for country-dwellers and country-lovers alike. For an authentic appreciation of these problems we must turn to the archives of an organization such as the Council for The Protection of Rural England* which in the inter-war period carried out innumerable studies on litter, pollution, rural electrification, afforestation, green belts and town and country planning. Concerns of this nature heralded the countryside of the future, a more managed, state-directed, enterprise – relatively prosperous, democratic and accessible, a social amenity of outstanding value within the powerhouse of the industrial state.

References

The following works have been quoted and drawn upon in the Introduction, one of the aims of which has been to summarize the existing state of academic knowledge on this period.

Collins, unpublished: a number of important, but as yet unpublished articles by Dr E. J. T. Collins (Director of the Institute of Agricultural History, University of Reading) was consulted.

Dewey, unpublished: *Farm Labour in Wartime*, unpublished Ph.D. thesis by Peter Dewey, was the source of the specific information in the caption to Plate 5. University of Reading, 1978.

Tracy, 1982: *Agriculture in Western Europe: Challenge and Response 1880–1980*, by Michael Tracy. London: Granada.

Whetham, 1978: *The Agrarian History of England and Wales, volume 8, 1919–1939*, by Edith Whetham. Cambridge: Cambridge University Press. Whetham was a general source for some of the captions.

* The title of the organization changed to this in 1969; it archives are held by the Institute of Agricultural History University of Reading.

Notes on Photographic Sources

Miss M. Wight (1889–1973) From her Worcester schooldays, Miss Wight was a prolific amateur photographer. She concentrated on recording buildings, and disappearing crafts and agricultural practices, from the West Country to Yorkshire and East Anglia, but especially in South Wales, the Cotswolds, Worcestershire and Herefordshire. Her photographs appear in many books, including K. S. Woods's *Rural Crafts of England* (1949). She lived at Mordiford and then Hereford: her photographs are held by the Institute of Agricultural History, University of Reading; Hereford City Library; the Welsh Folk Museum, St Fagans, Cardiff, and by the National Monuments Record. Miss Wight's personality comes across in a letter of 1964 sent to the University of Reading:

> Here is another selection of my old negatives and please feel free to destroy any not worth filing. I expect you know that the last of the Welsh turners' shops has come to an end; the Davies of Abercynch; the place was burnt and not even insured. A great loss.

Eric Guy Professional photographer in partnership with P. O. Collier of Reading from mid-1920s until about 1940, Guy subsequently set up in business on his own account, styling himself a press photographer. From the late 1920s his work appeared in the farming press, depicting agricultural scenes in Berkshire, South Oxfordshire, Hampshire and Wiltshire. Guy was particularly good at showing horses at work, and recorded mechanization in the thirties. His collection is held by the Institute of Agricultural History, University of Reading.

Farmer and Stock-Breeder The collection includes some 150,000 glass negatives and prints taken between the late 1920s and the 1970s. Subjects covered include arable and livestock farming; prevailing husbandry practices, the introduction of new techniques and the application of science to agriculture. There is an interesting series recording visits to farms carried out after 1930, as well as a series taken at the main agricultural shows after 1928. Photographs taken before the late 1920s have not survived. The collection is held by the Institute of Agricultural History, University of Reading.

Farmers' Weekly Consisting of some 20,000 glass negatives and prints taken between 1934 and the 1970s, the collection covers much the same ground as *Farmer and Stock-Breeder*, but with greater emphasis on events and personalities. The collection is held by the Institute of Agricultural History, University of Reading.

A Note on the Commentaries

Places are located within the county boundaries which existed at the time of photography, and no account has been taken in the text of the local government reorganization of 1974. For a few photographs the place is unknown but all are believed to have been taken in England. The book does not attempt to cover Scotland and Wales. A considerable number of photographs are precisely dated; in other cases an approximate estimate of the date has been established from internal evidence.

9 *Right* Cable cultivation by steam ploughing engines. The heavy five-furrow anti-balance plough was hauled backwards and forwards across the field by the winding drums under the boilers of two Fowler engines. At the end of each furrow they moved forward along the headland and the plough was reversed and drawn back up the field, weighed down into the soil with three men in addition to the steersman. At the beginning of the war the Steam Cultivation Development Association was urging farmers to make greater use of cable tackle operated by contractors to break up new or derelict land for cultivation or to prepare it for spring-sown crops. With the ending of the plough-up policy of the First World War and the inter-war depression in arable farming, the number of steam ploughing sets in use had declined from 600 in 1918 to 125 in 1938. Photograph by Eric Guy in central southern England, April 1940.

Hay and Corn

10 *Top* Ploughman 'riding' his plough around the headland of a field. This is a double-furrow plough drawn by three horses. Although it needed greater skill and strength on the part of the ploughman it was more economical in operation than two single-furrow ploughs requiring two men and four horses for their draught. On light and medium soils the double furrow plough was the most efficient means of employing horse power. Photograph by Eric Guy in central southern England, February 1939.

11 *Above* Drilling wheat on the Lockinge estate, Berkshire. This is the traditional type of steerage or Suffolk drill. It was heavy of draught, requiring three or four horses, and expensive of labour, employing a carter, a man behind the forecarriage to keep the fore-wheels aligned to the rear wheels to ensure the drilling of straight rows, and another man behind the drill to check that the seed was dropping freely and evenly through the coulters. Photograph by Eric Guy, *c.* 1939.

2 A break during haymaking in a park landscape in ntral southern England. The horse rake was uployed to gather the cut swaths into windrows for ying. The haymakers are still using the traditional rush basket to carry their food and drink but also have a modern vacuum flask to provide them with hot tea in the field. Photograph by Eric Guy.

23

13 *Left* Stacking hay near Amersham, Buckinghamshire. One of the last surviving uses of the portable horse gear during this period was to power the stack elevator.

14 *Left, below* Harvesting wheat with a self-binder in central southern England. First introduced about 1880, the self-binder had replaced the earlier self-delivery (or sail reaper) virtually everywhere by 1920. It cut and gathered the corn and discharged it in bound sheaves. This was the most complex horse-drawn implement of the farm yet the power for all its operations was solely derived from the rotating of its land wheel as it was drawn across the field. Note the home-made whip attached to this small binder. Photograph by Eric Guy.

15 Shocking wheat sheaves to dry in Buckinghamshire. The replacement of the binder by the combine harvester since 1950 has led to the disappearance in our time of both corn shocks (or stooks) and hay and corn ricks (or stacks).

16 Pitching barley into a harvest wagon at Compton, Berkshire. The capacity of this small, probably factory-built, wagon was increased by fitting a ladder at the front end. Photograph by Eric Guy.

17 Threshing crew having their meal against a shelter of loose straw and bagged grain at Cholsey Five Ways, Berkshire. The separate threshing machine, powered by a steam traction engine or a tractor, has also been supplanted by the combine harvester, which threshes the corn immediately after reaping it. The set of threshing tackle with its driver and his mate was normally supplied by contractors, the unthreshed grain being stored in the stack until their arrival. Photograph by Eric Guy.

18 More sophisticated threshing equipment at the farm
of R. W. N. Dawe, Alrewas Haye, Burton-on-Trent,
Staffordshire. A Ransomes traction engine drives a
threshing machine (also probably by Ransomes or
Ruston) connected to a Ruston baler. At this period
balers manufactured by Ruston & Hornsby of Lincoln
were marketed by Ransomes, Sims and Jefferies of
Ipswich. The unthreshed corn is stored loose in the
Dutch barn into which the straw bales are also loaded.
The labourer by the machine is clearing away the chaff
which has accumulated underneath it.

Potatoes and Vegetables

19 Women field workers planting potatoes in the newly opened furrows. The long rows of identical houses behind demonstrate the encroachment of suburbia upon the market garden areas which surrounded the great conurbations.

20 Filling the tank of a Gratton sprayer with a Solignum product to spray potatoes (in the right-hand field) against Colorado beetle on S. Gunary & Sons' farm, Rainham, Essex in August 1933. The pump of the power sprayer was operated by the Lister engine to the left of the tank. The seven-row brass spraying tubes and their connecting rubber pipes are folded in the travelling position. Dry powder was mixed with water from the tank mounted on the cart and the liquid was subsequently transferred into the sprayer-tank by buckets. The firm of D. T. Gratton of Boston, Lincolnshire, was established as a blacksmith's business in 1895 and manufactured spraying equipment from 1911 until the mid-1950s. In the background is an incomplete electricity pylon of the new national grid then being strung across the country.

21 Women sorting potatoes from a newly opened clamp at St Mary Cray, Kent, 1935. A tarpaulin sheet has been set up to gain some protection from the cold wind. Photograph by John Topham.

22 *Below* Using dibbers to plant rows of Brussels sprouts seedlings near Evesham, Worcestershire in April 1932. Both leather gaiters and the rubber wellington boots which were to replace them are worn by the labourers here.

23 *Right* Record harvest of Savoy cabbages, on a farm near Plympton, south Devon, September 1937. The wicker crates are loaded on to a lorry for the Plymouth market.

24 *Right, below* Women pea pickers at West Malling, Kent. The picking baskets are inspected before being emptied into market baskets.

25 Cutting the first of the summer
crop of watercress into baskets from
the beds of Mrs M. Simmons, a
specialized grower of South Darenth
near Dartford, Kent, May 1935.
Note the market chip basket into
which watercress was packed.
Photograph by John Topham.

Fruit and Hops

26 Spraying dessert apples against scab with lime-sulphur in a Kent orchard, late April 1932. The labourers' ragged clothing is probably adequate protection against this particular mixture applied by the power sprayers.

27 *Left, above* 'Pulling plums'. The picking baskets are emptied directly into the chip baskets, ready for sale. In the inter-war years considerable attention was paid to the packing and marketing of fruit and Government reports recommended the use of chips to prevent the crushing and loss of bloom and colour caused by transport in the traditional bushel or half-bushel baskets. A light picking ladder is used to prevent damage to the sensitive branches of the plum tree. Most English plums were grown in Kent and the Vale of Evesham.

28 *Left* Strawberry picking commences at St Mary Cray, Kent, June 1934. It was thought that owing to the drought and an attack of mite a poor crop would result, but returns revealed that the fruit was good and plentiful. The crates of strawberry chips are about to be loaded by the pickers on to a lorry, bound for the London market.

29 Hop picking bin being emptied, via the bushel measuring basket, into the poke for transport to the kiln. These pickers are working on the farm of M. Lewis, at Cranbrook, Kent in September 1932. In that year the acreage of English hops fell by 3,000 acres from the 1931 figure to reach 16,000 acres, the lowest thus far on record apart from the wartime year of 1918.

30 Aerial view of hop picking at Wellington, Herefordshire. The picking bins and wirework supporting the hop bines may be clearly seen. About 50 men, women and children are visible in the photograph, a reminder of the amount of labour required to harvest hops before picking machines became generally available after the Second World War.

New Machines

31 This photograph taken at a machinery demonstration held at Hathern, near Loughborough, Leicestershire in 1937, shows the difficulty of adjusting the self-lift trailed tractor plough in operation. The Fordson tractor is a model N showing the tapering toolboxes of the Cork-built models of 1930–31, but it has unusual non-standard rear wheels. The three-furrow plough with disc coulters is a Cockshutt, probably a no. 4 or no. 6 tractor plough. Since 1931 the English agents of this Canadian firm, R. A. Lister of Dursley, Gloucestershire had publicized the plough by offering farmers free demonstrations in the field.

32 Ferguson-Brown tractor with a row crop cultivator working on a crop of spring cabbage in 1937. This lightweight tractor, designed by Harry Ferguson, was manufactured, with its new range of mounted implements, by David Brown of Huddersfield from 1936. It introduced for the first time in the tractor the principle of the hydraulic lift with draught control and the converging three-point linkage; light implements had their depth of soil penetration, raising and lowering controlled by a hydraulic system which automatically compensated for irregularities or obstructions in the ground. This was immediately accepted as a major advance in tractor design. Production of this tractor was terminated in 1939 after 1,350 had been built and the two parties went their own way, Ferguson to co-operate with Henry Ford in the production of the Ford 9N (Ferguson system) tractor and David Brown to become one of the leading British tractor manufacturers using most of Ferguson's revolutionary principles.

3 *Left* The new American Oliver 70-row crop tractor n the Davidson and Logsdon farm, Great Barford, edfordshire in 1936. The three-row ridging plough is ttached to a centrally mounted rigid frame and is seen ere covering up the ridges after the planting of otatoes. The row crop concept was developed by nternational Harvester in the 1920s but was never as opular in Britain as in the United States. The very arrow spade lugs on the rear wheels of the tractor were esigned not only to secure maximum adhesion but so to stir the soil at the same time.

34 A 44 hp P-type Lanz Bulldog crude oil tractor and a Cockshutt three-furrow plough being demonstrated at Saxham, Bury St Edmunds, Suffolk in 1936. The tractor belonged to Barnard-Smith, contractors of Church Hall, Wood Ditton, Cambridgeshire. This German tractor had a single-cylinder semi-diesel engine with hot bulb ignition, dispensing with valves, carburettor and magneto. Bulldogs were highly praised by the Hosier brothers (writing in 1951): '... their extreme simplicity and longevity has been proved beyond question. Until the war became imminent we purchased no other make of tractor. The first, purchased in 1929, has not yet reached the scrapheap.' In the background is a Lanz crawler tractor.

35 *Left* An International Harvester Farmall tractor on the farm of R. Crouch, Teffont Magna, Wiltshire in May 1934. The two grain drills are crudely attached with single pole hitches. The Farmall, which appeared in the USA at the end of the 1920s, was designed with a high ground clearance for use with directly mounted implements over growing crops.

36 *Left, below* Fitting a rubber-tyred wheel to a Fordson tractor at the field station of the University of Oxford, Institute for Agricultural Research, Long Wittenham, Berkshire in August 1939. The tractor, a Land Utility model introduced in 1934, is fitted with headlights, horn and rear view mirror and normally had rubber tyres as standard equipment. Pneumatic tyres for farm tractors were introduced into Britain by Dunlop in 1933. The cleated or spade-lug wheels previously used on tractors, although giving a very good grip on the soil, damaged the road surface unless modified and thus restricted the mobility of the tractor. The low-pressure inflatable tractor tyre had the ability to grip as well as the steel rims but was also smoother in operation. Pneumatic tyres were increasingly offered by tractor manufacturers from the mid-thirties and were fitted to many older tractors.

37 Lifting early potatoes with a spinner behind an Allis-Chalmers Model U tractor on Bowerman's Farm, Wick, near Littlehampton, West Sussex in 1938. The Model U had been used by Allis-Chalmers to introduce the first American pneumatic tractor tyres in 1932. These had been manufactured by Firestone like the examples fitted to this tractor. This potato digger or spinner fitted with rotary forks driven by the land wheels of the implement was developed in the late nineteenth century. An operational disadvantage was its tendency to throw the potatoes out some distance, making it more difficult for the pickers to collect them (hence the net attached on the right).

8 *Left, above* Liming in Berkshire from a Bedford two-ton truck of 1931–34 manufacture. The Bedford was one of the first commercial vehicles produced by Vauxhall Motors and in 1932 was being advertised at £250 as specially suited for farm work. The direct use of light commercial vehicles on the land had become increasingly common at this period. The lime was supplied from the kiln of F. Lovegrove of Theale, west of Reading. The method of operation is primitive with only eye goggles being worn by the labourers as protection against the corrosive effect of the quicklime. Photograph by Eric Guy.

39 *Left* This tractor adaptation of a standard Ford chassis was demonstrated on the farm of J. W. Brown of Moor Close, Ashbourne, Derbyshire c. 1936. It could be fitted with a variety of implements for row crop work or operate with normal tractor equipment. It is shown here haymaking with a side-delivery rake manufactured by Blackstone of Stamford, combining the swaths into windrows for collection. This particular implement, introduced about 1930, could also be employed as a swath turner, turning over the swaths to dry them on the other side. The use of cheap cars and trucks in haymaking had been pioneered by the Hosier brothers. Such vehicles were much cheaper and faster than tractors and in the thirties could be purchased second-hand for five or ten pounds.

40 Hay sweeps and a stacker at Compton, Berkshire. The tractors are the International 10–20 on the left (the wheels being fitted with over-tyres to protect the crop against the spade lugs) and an early International crawler, the T20, on the right. There was a great vogue for the hay-sweep, attached to tractor or car, in the inter-war years. It was developed from the horse sweep long used for hay collection in some areas of the country. Here the two sweeps are used in conjunction with the high-lift or overshot stacker, an American development, introduced in the 1920s. The tractor loads the arm of the stacker at ground level from the sweep. The cable is attached and the vehicle drives forward lifting up the arm of the stacker until the load is deposited on top of the stack. Photograph by Eric Guy.

41 Binder hauled by the larger International 15–30 tractor near Amesbury, Wiltshire. As the last portion of barley is cut, animals such as rabbits which have retreated to the centre of the field, bolt out and are chased by the boys. In the background is the Southern Railway branch line.

42 *Right* The Fowler rein-drive tractor under test near Leeds with a binder in October 1924. The design was patented by the Australian, Cornelius Murnane and first demonstrated in 1923. Although John Fowler & Co. Ltd of Leeds obtained the licence to manufacture this paraffin-engined tractor in Britain it was never a commercial success. It seemed a little absurd to offer the same sort of control for a tractor that was necessary for a team of horses, the reins allowing the driver to start, stop, go forward and backward and to brake and steer the tractor. In other respects the tractor design was sophisticated, allowing direct coupling to a variety of implements and possessing wheels of the rolling-pad or tracklaying type.

43 *Right, below* Ploughs and hay rakes awaiting dispatch outside the implement warehouse at Ransomes, Sims and Jefferies Ltd, Orwell Works, Ipswich, Suffolk in July 1919. The electric vehicle in the left background is one of Ransomes' own manufacture. Production of agricultural implements was still at a high level, swelled by the short-lived post-war boom. In the years of agricultural depression which followed, Ransomes placed an increasing emphasis on non-agricultural products including garden machinery, electric vehicles and vehicle bodies. Nevertheless the association of the firm with Ruston & Hornsby and the failure of its main rival, Howard of Bedford, helped to consolidate Ransomes' position as the premier British agricultural engineering company.

44 Trials of a Massey-Harris 9C harvester-thresher at the farm of J. P. Bragg, Headbourne Worthy, Hampshire in late August 1929. This 12-foot machine, designed for the Argentine market, had an auxiliary engine to power the machinery but was not self-moving. It is here hauled by a Wallis 20–30 tractor (the Wallis Tractor Co. of Cleveland Ohio became part of the Canadian Massey-Harris company in 1928). Although long employed in the world's major grain-producing areas, combine harvesters were not demonstrated in Britain until 1928. These trials were organized by the Institute for Research in Agricultural Engineering, University of Oxford and the University of Reading. A report stated that 'thistles abounded' in the 36-acre barley field. The crop on the right has been cut with the binder and shocked for drying before it is carted away for stacking and ultimate threshing. This was a task which the combine harvester, or harvester-

thresher as it was then known in Britain, performed with far greater economy in a single operation, the threshed grain being deposited in bags. Before harvesting the crop had to be completely ripe. The straw was collected up by a hay sweep and stacked, but it was necessary to dry the grain artificially as the moisture content was still too high for bulk storage. The combine did not play a significant role in British farming before the Second World War; the first

agricultural machinery census of the Ministry of Agriculture in 1942, revealed a total of 940 combines as against 101,970 binders.

45 The assembly line of Ferguson-Brown tractors at the David Brown gear factory, Huddersfield, West Riding of Yorkshire in 1937. All but the last twenty of the 1,350 built were produced at this works before the opening of the new tractor works at Meltham in 1939.

46 Using an electric light and extension cable to examine the underside of a wagon at E. G. Farmer's farm, Stanstead, Hertfordshire in 1936. The wagon was built (or repainted) by C. J. Butcher, wheelwright and agricultural engineer of Dunmow, Essex. The high cost of connecting outlying farms to the newly strung national grid, with transformers and service lines, induced some farmers to invest in motor-driven generating sets. This farm, however, was connected to the mains supply and electric motors were also used to raise water from deep wells and force it into a pressure tank.

Pest Control

47 Rabbit gassing near Welwyn, Hertfordshire, using the exhaust fumes of a saloon car.

48 A more traditional method of
vermin control. An Ipswich rat
catcher with his dogs, ferret and
ratting spade photographed during
National Rat Week, 1928. The dogs
located the rats and killed those
which escaped from bolt holes after
the ferret had been put down.

Livestock

49 Devon steers tackling their
fodder in the straw yard after a run
out on grass, at Mr E. F. Case's farm,
Withycombe, Washford, near
Taunton, Somerset, January 1939
(see also no. 142).

50 *Left* Swedes being cut into slices for winter feed, at the Norfolk Agricultural Station, Sprowston, November 1930. The root mill in the foreground is constructed of wood and powered by hand; it is of the same basic design as machines developed in the 1840s. Roots are fed into a hopper, where they press down on the cutting cylinder operated by a flywheel. Note the use of baskets to catch the sliced roots. Baskets were still made locally at this time and large numbers were supplied to market gardeners in the area. The root mill in the background was manufactured by Nicholson's of Newark on Trent, Nottinghamshire.

51 *Left, below* Silage-making in a pit, at a demonstration at the Farm Institute, Sparsholt, near Winchester, Hampshire, June 1934. The process used is the AIV system, introduced from Finland. Grassland herbage was packed into silos of wood, concrete or steel. Mineral acid was added to inhibit bacterial action and the surface was then commonly sprayed to prevent mould growth. This method of conserving grass was efficient, but filling the silo was laborious and handling strong acid was unpopular with the workers. It was also necessary, when the silage was fed, to neutralize the acid by adding ground chalk.

52 Grass drying demonstration at Berwick Farm, Fonthill Bishop, Wiltshire, May 1936, recorded by the *Farmer and Stock-Breeder*.

By the 1930s haymaking was often condemned as old-fashioned and wasteful, and agricultural scientists urged the commercial development of substitute processes, including artificial grass drying. The method of drying a crop was to pass hot air over and through the wet grass, which was placed on a tray, or moveable band, or cascaded in a revolving drum. The machine shown here is a large Billingham drier, made by ICI. The grass was dried for 20 minutes at a temperature of 150° centigrade and then made into bales, each weighing 100 lbs. The management of grass for drying was, however, more complicated than expected and the Agricultural Research Council commented in 1937 that it seemed likely that grass drying would develop as a semi-factory trade, rather than as part of the normal routine of farming. It was not only the driers which were expensive to install and to operate; handling short grass required special machinery, such as the Wilder 'Cutlift' developed for this task, and the capital cost could not be covered from the spring flush of grass on ordinary dairy farms.

The tractor shown in the photograph is an International 10–20.

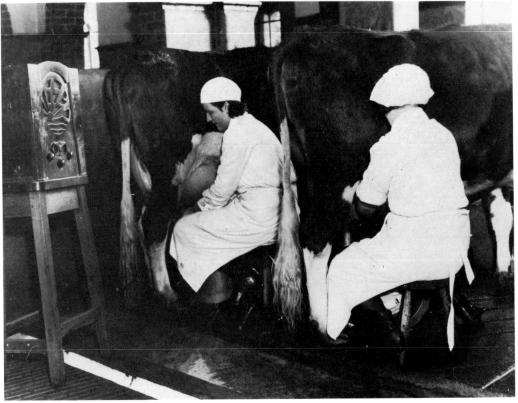

53(a) & (b) These photographs show the increased attention to cleanliness, even in hand milking, in this period. The milkers are wearing white overalls and a head covering, while the men are also wearing rubber boots.

The top photograph shows scrubbing up before milking. The milk pail in the doorway is a 'Davies' Sanitary Pail, made of tinned plate and designed to ensure that no dirt could fall into the milk during milking. Its capacity was 14 quarts and the Dairy Supply Co. Ltd, London, advertised such pails at 19/6d each in their 1924 catalogue: it was the most expensive of the various pails for milking, carrying and dairy work.

The lower photograph is interesting in showing the early use of the radio to provide music to soothe the cows and perhaps the milkmaids too. Taken at Sir John Leigh's Guernsey Dairy at Witley Park, near Godalming, Surrey, about 1930. The photographer in both cases was Eric Guy.

54 Open-air milking on the farm of Mr J. Balding, Nutley Manor, Basingstoke, Hampshire, August 1938. The bail system was developed by the Hosier brothers in the mid-1920s as a means of turning out high-quality milk without being involved in the expense of a cowhouse, and allowed dairy herds to be run on poor downland. Continued treading by the cattle and the even distribution of dung improved the quality of the pasture. Moreover, the milk was free from contamination from airborne bacteria and dust particles, as from the moment it left the cow until it was deposited in the churn it was in a vacuum. The disadvantages of the system were the bad weather conditions under which men had to work in winter and the difficulty of controlling feed, calving and yields. It was also sometimes a problem to get enough water to clean cows and equipment. Note the fly spray on the roof! The system was suitable only for herds of moderate yields, although Mr Balding considered that an average of 657 gallons for his 68 Ayrshires satisfactory – particularly in view of the low costs of production.

55 *Left* Milking with a 'Alfa-Laval' combine plant, the first of its kind to be installed in Britain, at the Clyde Higgs farm, Hatton Rock, Stratford on Avon, Warwickshire, October 1934. The cowhouse was a low, four-span Dutch barn. In the front spans were the sterilizing plant, dairy and milking stand, and the feeding standings with room for the 120 pedigree Ayrshires were directly behind this. Here the cows were washed and groomed, before making their own way to the milking stands – where they were kept in place by a chain around their quarters. After milking, the attendant pulled a cable, which opened a gate in front of the cow, and she returned to the feeding quarters, but by a separate route. The milk yield was an average of 800 gallons per cow, a good performance at this time. During the 1930s, however, the 'thousand gallon' cow ceased to be a rarity and by the end of the decade, there were three cows which had each topped 3000 gallons in a single lactation.

56 *Left, below* The 'brand-boy' marking a newly-sheared sheep with a brand that has been dipped in Stockholm tar – a scene at the annual sheep-shearing of Blackfaces that roam the Cheviot hills, Northumberland, August 1932. The Blackface breed is outstanding in harsh conditions and, with the Cheviot, came to dominate upland sheep farming in this area.

57 Sheep-dipping, carried out to control parasitic infestations of sheep, under the Sheep Scab Orders of the Ministry of Agriculture. Taken in Yorkshire, July 1937.

Successful dipping depends on lowering the sheep gently into the fluid, so that it does not draw a mouthful of dip into the stomach or lungs, and also on ensuring that the whole of the fleece is immersed. The sheep is kept on the move, with the use of the crutch to help the penetration of the dip through the fleece. The best time to carry out dipping is in fine, cool weather, never on a hot or sultry day or in thundery weather, or when rain is expected. It should be carried out so that the sheep have time to dry before the hottest part of the day and certainly before nightfall.

58 Sheep-shearing: Mr. C. Fowler of Alveston, at work on Mr W. S. Read's farm at Almondsbury, Gloucestershire May 1936. The shears are being worked from a belt driven by the rear wheel of a motor van, which has been raised from the ground.

59 *Far left* Shepherd Jimmy Dunford, in a blizzard, December 1937. He claimed to be, at 71, the oldest working shepherd on Salisbury plain. A week earlier, the Wiltshire shepherds had their tenth Christmas supper at Marlborough Town Hall. At this Mr H. W. Tomlinson, the assistant county organizer for agriculture, urged the advantages of the traditional system of folding flocks on arable land, although many shepherds now had charge of grass flocks. At this time arable flocks, such as the Hampshire Downs, were becoming less profitable, even though sheep folded on a root break increased the productivity of the succeeding corn crops.

60 *Left* A fresh outbreak of foot-and-mouth disease in the winter and spring of 1937/8 led to the imposition of the most drastic standstill order since 1922, restricting the movements of cattle in all but six counties of England. Nearly 1,000 surgeons in the 78 new centres of the State Veterinary Service were involved. In some centres, markets had to be closed and thousands of livestock slaughtered. The photograph shows Ben Ward, the local slaughterman, dipping his feet in disinfectant when entering Little Highfield Farm at Ravensden, near Bedford, April 1938.

61 Clipping out a workhorse, Mylor, near Falmouth, Cornwall, November 1937. The hand-powered machine was driven by a handle connected to a flywheel and gearbox at the top of the tubular stand. The cutting blades were adjustable and hair could be left up to 5/16″ in length.

62 Ground cereals being fed to Large White pigs, May 1939. The profitability of pig-farming was a perennial question. *Farmers' Weekly* declared, in an accompanying article: 'If a party of farmers are talking "shop" and if you want to hear lively discussion, there is probably no more certain way of provoking it than by launching the question "Does pig farming pay". It is highly probable that the question will be met with the direct assertion that pigs lose £1 apiece for fattening. But after some hesitation someone else will venture the opinion that he makes nearer £1 a pig profit than £1 a pig loss. The link between these two very opposite opinions is summed up in the word – management.'

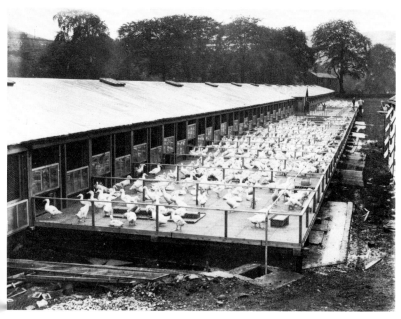

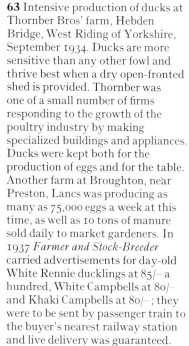

63 Intensive production of ducks at Thornber Bros' farm, Hebden Bridge, West Riding of Yorkshire, September 1934. Ducks are more sensitive than any other fowl and thrive best when a dry open-fronted shed is provided. Thornber was one of a small number of firms responding to the growth of the poultry industry by making specialized buildings and appliances. Ducks were kept both for the production of eggs and for the table. Another farm at Broughton, near Preston, Lancs was producing as many as 75,000 eggs a week at this time, as well as 10 tons of manure sold daily to market gardeners. In 1937 *Farmer and Stock-Breeder* carried advertisements for day-old White Rennie ducklings at 85/- a hundred, White Campbells at 80/- and Khaki Campbells at 80/-; they were to be sent by passenger train to the buyer's nearest railway station and live delivery was guaranteed.

64 Fattening Christmas turkeys the traditional way. The birds are being fed on barley gleanings, on a poultry farm near Stevenage, Hertfordshire, September 1935.

65 Chick 'sexer' at work on the Somerset Accredited Breeders' Hatchery at Bathpool, in January 1939. The quickness and deftness of the Japanese made them experts at determining the sex of chicks – a matter relatively easy to establish in 80 per cent of the chicks, although skill and experience was called for in dealing with the remaining 20 per cent. At this station, the incubators held 65,000 eggs at any one time. During the 1920s poultry production was still quite profitable, due to low feeding costs and satisfactory prices. The industry expanded rapidly but increased egg production, coupled with plentiful foreign supplies, reduced profits in the 1930s. A sharp rise in the cost of feed after 1936 brought hardship to many producers. Small farmers in particular responded by raising more fowls from poorer stock, leading to an alarming increase in disease. One way of combating this was the Accredited Poultry Breeding Scheme; accredited hatcheries guaranteed to supply healthy chicks to producers. By 1939, five such stations had been established in different parts of the country.

Manor Farm, Notgrove

The photographs in this group are from the family album of Mr P. Webster Cory, who farmed at Manor Farm, Notgrove, Bourton-on-the-Water, Gloucestershire, from 1916. The farm, which comprised some 1,000 acres in the 1930s, was originally a typical arable farm, but was converted to grass during the inter-war period. There were four enterprises: dairying on the Hosier principle of open-air milking bails, grass sheep for fat lamb production, pigs for bacon, and poultry for egg production. Each of these departments was an entirely separate unit capable of expansion or contraction at a moment's notice and of being accurately cost-accounted so that its value to the whole could be checked. The secret of the farm's success, however, lay in the business flair and organizing ability of Mr Cory himself. The first seven photographs were taken between 1918 and 1923, the last three in the mid-1930s.

6 The two-cylinder tractor is an Overtime, Model N, known in the United States as the Waterloo Boy. It was originally manufactured by the Waterloo Gasoline Engine Co. and later by John Deere. Nearly 20,000 Type Ns were produced from 1917 to 1924. In Britain it was distributed by the Associated Manufacturers Co. of London and cost £368 in 1919. With the Fordson, International Titan and Mogul it was one of the most successful US tractors in Britain. Here, it is seen with a hut made on the property used for carrying equipment, and as a shelter. The plough appears to be a four-furrow Overtime.

67 Mrs Dorothy Cory and her daughter Pamela, in the Glebe garden.

68 Mr Webster Cory and his horse Charlie

The Manager, Mr Wetton (centre); with Jessup, pig
unit (seated, right); and three farm pupils, Swainson
(seated, left), Castell (standing, left) and Rydon
(standing, right). Later, Wetton was to move to
another employment but died young; Jessup joined an
animal feed firm; Castell became a tenant farmer at
Chipping Norton, and Rydon took a farm at
Sherbourne. What happened to Swainson is unknown.

70 Spreading dung from a tip-cart. Shepherd Miles and his dog are on the right of the photograph and the man in the centre, called Creed, was employed in hedging and ditching during the winter months. Fred Dancer is holding the horse's head.

71 *Left* Feeding the pigs. The herd seems to be Large and Middle White crosses. The stockman is Fred Finchin senior; his son Fred was senior dairyman on No. 1 dairy (Hosier-type, of which there were three). At first herds were kept in the open air, but by the mid-1920s the system was to keep fattening pigs under cover. By then, different rations were mixed for separate age groups and categories of pigs, and the manure was returned to the grassland to be dealt with by means of mechanical dung-spreaders.

72 The store house, where all the different foods and meals were kept. The rations were mixed in bulk on the top floor and placed ready for use on the lower floor under the name of the stock for which they were intended. Thence they were fetched by the stockman concerned, who marked up the quantity removed until the week's allocation had been drawn. The man shown on the left of the photograph is George Mace; the other man is unknown.

73 Hosier milking bail. The milkman, Fred Pinchin Junior, is filling a churn with milk which has been passed through a cooling tank; the water is drawn from one water cart and returned to another to be re-used elsewhere. The dairy herd which numbered about 200 cows was divided into three units. One unit consisted of Ayrshires, another of Irish shorthorns and the third was a mixture of the two breeds. The whole herd produced about 90,000 gallons of milk a year, giving an average of 450–500 gallons per cow. The Hosier system was adopted at Notgrove Farm in October 1927.

74 This is one of three moveable laying units for poultry, each consisting of about 60 pens containing approximately 1,500 birds in the charge of one man. The hens were mainly Rhode Island Reds and Light Sussex crosses. The system isolated birds in small groups to limit the risk of disease, and prevented the depredations of foxes so that poultry could be run in fields next to coverts; furthermore, the pens could be moved daily across the field to achieve an even manuring of the turf. At the end of the day the eggs were collected and brought back to the egg store. The tractor is a Fordson, made at Cork in Ireland between 1929 and 1932 before production commenced at Dagenham. This Cork N model has pneumatic tyres, available from 1934. In the centre left of the photograph, Mr Cory is standing behind his sheepdog Spot.

75 Here the eggs are being washed and packed before being collected by the National Mark Egg-Packing Station at Cheltenham. Note the packet of 'Rinso', which promised a 'Rich Lasting Lather for every type of wash'!

Agricultural Shows

76 The Royal Agricultural Society of England annual show, date unknown. Until the late nineteenth century, agricultural shows frequently included trials of new machinery that appeared to onlookers to be gladiatorial contests between rival manufacturers and which succeeded, as often as not, in demonstrating the defects as much as the merits of the equipment being tested. As other means of communicating technical information became more important, agricultural shows came to fulfil a less pioneering and more limited function – although they still provided sellers with a valuable opportunity to attract buyers and, after the first day or so of trade attendance, casual visitors with an entertaining day out. The Royal Show remained the premier event in the show calendar and during this period was held at a different location each year. Attendance fluctuated considerably in the 1930s, but it was only in the worst of the Depression years – 1931 and 1932 – that the Show actually made a loss.

77 The *Farmer and Stock-Breeder* van at the Three Counties Show at Worcester, June 1933.

The farming press played a key role in the diffusion of new knowledge – through short articles contributed by agricultural experts, through reports on farm visits and reviews of the latest scientific and technical developments, and through their numerous pages of advertisements. Weeklies such as *Farmer and Stock-Breeder* (from 1889), and *Farmers' Weekly* (from 1934) were read by many, perhaps most, farm families, while local papers also provided market reports, notices of farm sales and articles of agricultural interest.

78 *Right* The Duke and Duchess of York at the Jubilee Show of the Hertfordshire Agricultural Society, June 1929. The Duke was President of the Society and presented the awards; there was a record number of entries – the total being 2,247, against 1,925 the previous year.

79 *Right, below* Shorthorn bull, exhibited by Sir B. Greenwell at the Smithfield Show, London, November 1932.

80 Suffolk shearling ewes at the Royal Show, Southampton, 1932.

81 *Below* Prize-winning Savoys – widely known as the Dutch cabbage – at the Loughborough Machinery Demonstration, Leicestershire, 1937.

82 *Right* A champion cockerel gets a beauty bath before meeting the judges at the National Dairy Show in London. Taken at Mr Borthwick's farm at Hatfield, Hertfordshire in October 1936.

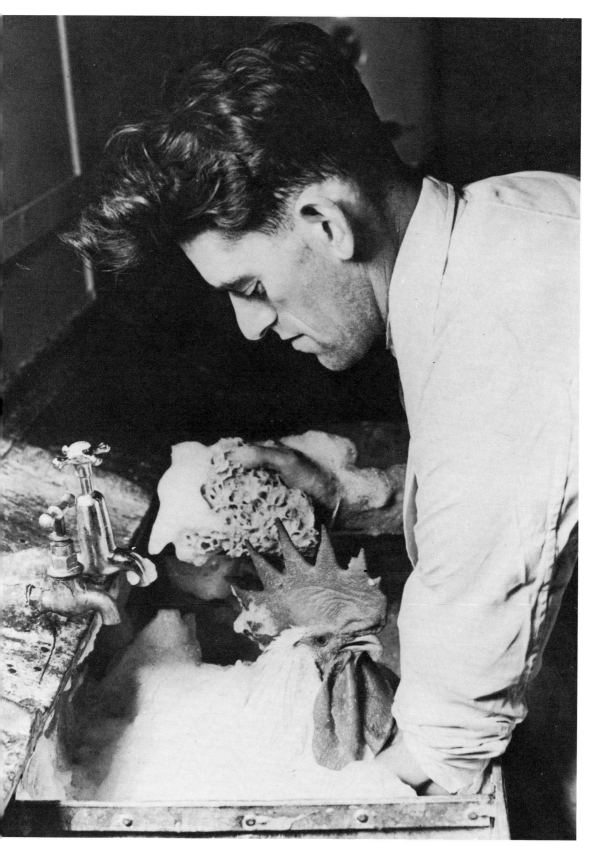

83 Imperial Fruit Show, Leicester, November 1934. Among the firms exhibiting canned fruit and vegetables are LinCan, Chivers, Smedleys, Bairds, Sandrings, Merrie England and Masons.

84 *Right* Traditional French onion sellers, François Damclou and Henri Fontes, on their 16th annual visit to England to sell onions. They made their headquarters at Bristol and are seen here on their daily round, at Cam, Gloucestershire. Taken in September 1937.

Marketing

85 Milk delivery. A. D. Woodley and Son, Little John's Farm, Oxford Road, Reading, Berkshire, commenced retailing milk to the borough, with a population of about 100,000, in 1929. By registering as a Grade A producer and selling best-quality milk – for which there was an increasing demand at the top end of the market – the firm was able to build up a round of from five to 22 gallons daily in three months. Paper cartons were a new idea at this time; the cost of the containers was about the same as glass, but the need for the elaborate sterilization of bottles was overcome. Customers, however, preferred glass bottles and many dairies returned to them. The photograph was taken in February 1930.

86 *Right* Miss Turner in her dairy, filling cartons of Grade A milk, June 1935. She had been a successful producer-retailer for a quarter-of-a-century, having established a herd of pedigree Ayrshires and Jerseys, which yielded between 60 and 70 gallons a day for sale in the Haywards Heath area, Sussex. Note the bunting in the window to mark the King's Jubilee and the commemorative supplement on the slatted shelves on the left. Among the various pieces of dairy equipment is a hand-cranked cream separator.

87 *Right, below* Mr J. R. Carter was one of a growing number of enterprising farmers in the 1930s who catered for the middle-class taste for 'country-fresh' foods. He started his Broad Oak Farm Sausage Company on a 200-acre mixed farm at Hatfield Broad Oak, Essex. Pure-bred Large White pigs produced a finished article with a high proportion of lean to fat. The bread-content of the sausages was baked locally and was yeast-free; special seasoning was added. The sausages were packaged and branded, then dispatched by Morris van or bicycle, or over greater distances by rail. Some were even sent on the maiden voyage of the Queen Mary. The photograph was taken in December 1936.

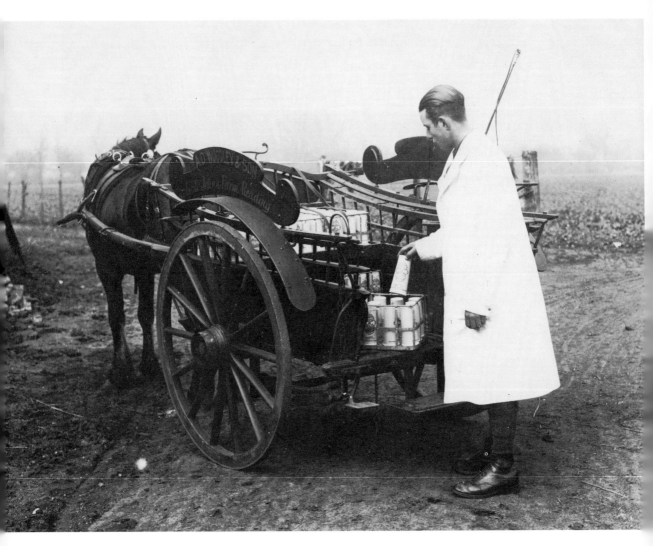

88 *Left* 'Health' foods, such as the heather honey shown here, found a ready sale among urban tourists, eager to visit newly opened country houses and gardens. This roadside shop was a small but profitable outlet on Lloyd George's property 'Bron-y-de', at Churt, Surrey. Of 250 acres of arable, 150 acres were planted with fruit trees, including Victoria plums and apples such as Cox's Orange Pippin, Bramley, Grenadier, Worcester and Newton Wonder. The farm employed a total of 40 men – ten on tending the fruit – at the above-average wage of 45/– a week. Taken in May 1937.

89 *Left, below* Reading Livestock Market, Berkshire, in the 1920s. The frequent sales of store and pedigree cattle were one of the most important functions of the market. The store cattle sales were arranged partly by firms of auctioneers and partly by the Country Gentlemen's Association (their enamel sign is on the side of the new cattle sale building). The Association paid special attention to the improvement of Irish store cattle sales. Before the sale, cattle in the pens were examined by representatives of the auctioneers and the

CGA. The bunches of cattle reaching a certain standard of quality were marked with a red ticket on the rump as a recommendation to buyers.

Note the temporary wooden pens erected alongside iron pens – a sign of the expansion of trade helped by Reading's excellent rail service to all parts of the country – the market adjoined the Great Western Railway. The other advertisements refer to Sutton Seeds; Goodenough's Ltd, corn and flour merchants; and to various firms of auctioneers – Hewett and Lee, Thimbleby and Shorland, F. W. Allwright and Son, and Simmons and Sons.

90 Devon steers being driven to the village fair and cattle market, Modbury, Devon, June 1934. The 600-year-old market was in danger of being closed as the cattle rendered the main street on the Plymouth arterial road almost impassable every market day. In the larger towns, markets had often been relocated to the outskirts of the town, near the railway station, both for the convenience of farmers and dealers and to avoid the health hazard caused by livestock periodically thronging the central thoroughfares.

91 The Shorthorn's Society's second spring show and sale of Dairy Shorthorn cows, heifers and bulls, at Reading Livestock Market, March 1938. A large number of buyers attended and prices ranged up to 100 guineas.

This photograph shows the interior of the new cattle-sale building shown on the previous page. Built of hollow terra-cotta brick, it had tiered sections for about 400 people. The ring was 20 ft in diameter and fitted with a 30-cwt dial weighbridge. It was used for sales of fat cattle and special sales of pedigree and store stock.

92 Barnham Market, West Sussex. The pigs are being marked by the butcher who has purchased them. In this case the mark is a cross made with a red wax pencil. The chief buyers were butchers from the towns and villages lying along or near the coast between Eastbourne and Portsmouth; occasionally buyers attended from London and Birmingham. In 1928 7,329 fat pigs and 2,616 store pigs were entered in the market, although it was more important for sales of fat cattle.

93 Old Covent Garden was the principal fruit and vegetable centre of Great Britain. Bulky vegetables were obtained from the Home Counties and from those districts where production was consistently in excess of local needs, such as Lincolnshire and Cambridgeshire for potatoes and Cornwall for broccoli. Home-grown fruit was also drawn from the Home Counties, particularly Kent and from other regularly exporting areas such as Cambridgeshire and Hampshire for strawberries and Devon and Hereford for apples. Imported fruits of all kinds were sold through Covent Garden, and provincial towns all over the country obtained their supplies from this market, particularly of the more expensive fruits.

Despite the lack of railway sidings, the total trade of Covent Garden expanded considerably in the 1920s, with the development of road transport. Indeed, the congestion in the area induced the Ministry of Transport to conduct a traffic census in 1926, which indicated that on one day, chosen at random, some 5,519 vehicles entered and 5,377 left the market. This photograph was taken during the 1930s and illustrates the problem at that time: note the horse-drawn wagon on the left which contrasts with the modern lorries – two types of Bedford, an Austin, a Foden and an Albion are visible.

An attempt was made to move the market in 1927 when the owners, the Covent Garden Properties Co. Ltd promoted a Bill to move it to Bloomsbury, but this was opposed by local trading associations and councils on the grounds of anticipated loss of revenue, and the Bill was dropped.

94 Smithfield market. The London Central Markets were established on the Smithfield site in 1868. Of the total supplies to the market in 1928 over 70 per cent was imported meat, delivered from the Docks; some 25 per cent was delivered by road and rail from outside of London, and the remaining 5 per cent came from slaughterhouses in the London area.

The market consisted of five separate buildings for the wholesale trade and two retail sections. Vehicles were not allowed to enter the market but, as shown in the photograph, were backed up to the whole length of external market pavement. There was room for 350 three-ton lorries to unload at a time. Market stalls were held on weekly tenancies, in return for the payment of a weekly rent, and tolls were collected from the carriers – motor transport firms, railways etc. – at the rate of $\frac{1}{4}$d for every 21 lb of all marketable commodities. Over 90 per cent of all the meat and poultry was sold to buyers in London and the Home Counties.

95 Office staff of the Milk Marketing Board, beginning the enormous task of registering some 140,000 milk producers, in August 1933. One problem was that many thousands of forms had to be sent back to farmers for correction. The Board had been set up the previous month to try to save many producers from bankruptcy. Increased imports of butter and cheese from 1929 pushed down prices, and as prices fell, farmers tried to sell more liquid milk, until supply exceeded demand. The Board's objectives were to stimulate the demand for liquid milk, to improve its quality, and to develop the market for manufactured milk products. It did much to create new marketing opportunities for dairy farmers in the 1930s.

96 Selling National Mark eggs, June 1936. Butter, poultry and eggs – traditionally sold by the women of farm households at local markets – varied greatly in quality. In 1928 the Ministry of Agriculture prescribed quality grades for British produce and licensed farmers, co-operative societies and dealers to use the 'National Mark' on graded commodities. By the following year, National Mark schemes were in operation for eggs; apples and pears; Cornish broccoli; and beef, sold in the wholesale markets of London and Birmingham. The eggs shown in this photograph were supplied by the Thames Valley Egg Packing Station, one of the few successful agricultural co-operatives of the inter-war period – it started trading in 1934.

97 Grading Worcester Pearmain apples at William Seabrook and Sons Ltd, fruit-growers and nurserymen, Chelmsford, Essex.

98 School children drinking Grade A milk, supplied by the Mawcroft Farm Dairy, Nether Yeadon, Leeds. The Government encouraged the milk drinking habit in the mid-1930s by providing free milk for all needy schoolchildren, while subsidizing it to others by selling to each child one third of a pint daily at school at the cost of one halfpenny, which was less than half the normal retail price of milk. 'Welfare' milk was also supplied to nursing and expectant mothers, and later the scheme was extended to areas of high unemployment in the North of England.

99 Milk bar, owned by J. Raymond Stovold, High Street, Godalming, Surrey, probably taken in 1938. A speciality was the Pure Dairy Cream Ices, made at Stovold's Eashing Farm Dairy, which won a Silver Medal at the Crystal Palace, 1936.

Milk bars became popular meeting places in the late 1930s, reflecting the new acceptance of milk as a high-status food, and the growing middle-class concern with health and a better diet. The first milk bar opened in London in 1935 and by the outbreak of the Second World War more than 1,300 were in business, encouraged by the Milk Marketing Board, which provided an advisory service to would-be proprietors.

Food Processing

100 Making butter, using an end-over-end churn, at Jesse Crumpler's farm, North Coker, near Yeovil, Somerset, March 1937. The farm supplied St Bartholomew's Hospital in London with 200 gallons of TT milk daily and in addition retailed another 100 gallons locally. There was also a large trade in butter and some sales of cream. The end-over-end churn was patented by William Waide and Sons, Leeds, in 1880.

Unlike ordinary barrel churns, the whole barrel was made to tumble by means of a hand crank, although in this case a small electric motor provided the power source, taking much of the toil out of the dairymaid's job. The churn worked best when only half-to-one-third full, but its chief advantage was that it was easier to clean than those with internal fittings.

101 A well-equipped dairy, at Rednal House Farm, Rednal, Worcestershire. Note the end-over-end churn, butter working table, butter pats and board in the right foreground, and the refrigerated store in the corner of the room. Taking notes is the owner, Mrs Butler, who was one of the first milk retailers to establish a Grade A dairy, which achieved a constant growth in milk sales to Birmingham. She was a subject for *Farmer and Stock-Breeder's* 'Successful Lady Farmer' series in December 1935.

102 Canning peas at the plant of W. P. Hartley, Aintree, Liverpool, August 1935. The peas were picked in the Ormskirk district, centre of the Lancashire potato industry. At the factory, they were shelled, winnowed, twice-washed and graded – then conveyed to an inspection table where poor specimens were removed. Afterwards they were canned, sealed and cooked and delivered at the rate of 90 cans a minute. Fruit and vegetable canning emerged as an important industry in the inter-war period. While only a handful of canneries had been established by the mid-1920s, more than 80 were recorded in a survey published in 1932, mainly in Kent and East Anglia. Until this time, the Americans led the way in canning technology, but British firms had considerably improved their produc by 1940.

103 Pressing cheeses at a dairy farm in Cheshire, June 1936. Cheese-making goes on from early May until late October. No cake is fed to the cattle during this time as the flavour of the cheese comes from the grass. Some fields will not make cheese while others are good in the spring but not in the autumn. Sheep should not be run over the land at the same time as cows, and nitrogenous top dressings must be avoided. After pressing, the cheese is bathed for one minute in water at 140°F, when the pores run together and a skin is formed. After numerous changes into fresh cloths, greasing with lard, and more pressing – the cheese is ready for three months in the ripening room, where it is turned every day for six weeks.

104 Sugar-beet factory at Bardney, Lincolnshire in the late 1920s. This factory, processing 2,000 tons of beet a day, and another at Brigg, were both owned by the Lincolnshire Sugar Beet Company. In 1925 the government sought to encourage the production of home-grown sugar by offering a subsidy to farmers to grow sugar beet. As a result the acreage expanded from some 23,000 acres in 1924 to more than 200,000 in 1927, mostly in East Anglia.

Farmers at first regarded sugar beet as a crop likely to impoverish the land, but experiments at the Norfolk Experimental Station showed that the beet crop, properly fertilized and with its residues fed to cattle or sheep, could raise yields of subsequent crops. Sugar beet thus provided a valuable opportunity for scientists and farmers to work together on the problems of cultivation, crop rotation, fertilizing and pest control. The actual process of production, however, was managed by the field staff of the 18 factories in existence by the end of the 1920s.

105 Making farm cider. The photograph shows ripe apples being crushed and pressed. The fruit is first 'mashed' in the small, hand-operated mill on the left, the pulp being collected in the open, wooden vat beneath. It is then packed into a 'cheese' built up of hair cloths, containing the pulp in layers. A board is placed on the cheese and a beam screwed down, compressing the cheese and forcing the juice to run out through the cloths, to collect in another vat at the foot of the press. Pressure is exerted through turning the screw by means of a pole acting as a lever. From the vat the juice would have been put into large hogsheads to ferment for a certain time, the impurities escaping with the froth that rises through the hole left open at the top. Finally it is corked up and laid away to mature. New cider is fierce and raw and is best left for at least six months.

Rural Industries

106 Small stone quarry in the Cotswolds. The pit has been cut by hand out of an open field site. This quarry appears to be producing both thin roofing slates (in the near pile) and larger building stones (in the pile behind). Photograph by Miss M. Wight.

107 The photographer and the rural worker. Miss M. Wight, photographing a charcoal burner at Flaxley, Gloucestershire in the Forest of Dean. The wooden barrow was used for a variety of purposes on the site, including the carriage of cordwood to the clamp, of paraffin as here and of the personal possessions of the burners who lived in turf shelters during the firing period.

108 *Right* Charcoal burning in Epping Forest, Essex in April 1939. The burners are cutting hornbeam and birch in front of the iron kilns, provided by the Timber Supplies Department of the Forestry Commission, which replaced the earth clamps. After the wood had been burning for 24 hours, the vents were closed to stop combustion. This was the first time that charcoal had been burnt in Epping for 40 years. The issue of gas masks, in which charcoal was used as a filter, to the entire population before the start of the war had helped to bring about a revival in the charcoal-burning industry.

109 Charles Glasspool completing a wattle hurdle at Eartham, West Sussex in March 1938. The uprights are inserted into a frame and both round and cleft hazel rods are interwoven between them. Glasspool is just pulling the finisher twice round the outside stake before tucking it in. A space is left in the centre of the hurdle for carrying it. A skilled hurdle maker could produce a wattle hurdle from previously cleft rods in twenty minutes. In spite of the decline in the number of flocks grazing on the arable and the increasing use of wire for folding, there was still a demand for closely woven wattle hurdles in south-east England to provide shelter in the lambing yard. Photograph by G. G. Garland.

95

110 Part of the hoop-maker's workshop of F. W. Backshall of Paddock Wood, Kent in January 1939. Such workshops were sited in or very close to the coppice woods from which the poles, commonly hazel, were cut. The split hoop length was gripped in the break as the hoop maker used the draw knife to shape it. An average worker could make about 400 hoops in a twelve-hour day. Note that the shelter is thatched with wood shavings. The coiled hoops were bundled for use in dry cooperage work which included the manufacture of barrels for apples, jam, salt, fish and gunpowder.

111 Making trug baskets at the premises of Thomas Smith & Son, Herstmonceux, Sussex. The firm was founded about 1830 and the workshop produced a hundred dozen baskets a month. The left-hand worker is shaping the willow strips with the draw knife on a 'horse'. A variety of completed trugs may be seen on the left. The rim and handle of the trug are made from cleft ash or chestnut rods, steamed and bent into two ovals. The willow strips are pressed into the framework so that they overlap with each other and are fixed by nails to the rim. Herstmonceux and Hailsham were the centres of the industry from which these gardeners' baskets were distributed all over Britain. Photograph by G. G. Garland.

112 Albert Carter, chain-leg turner, in his workshop at the Cherry Tree Inn, Stoke Row, Oxfordshire, October 1937. Carter is using the primitive pole lathe – the foot treadle was attached to a springy pole by means of a cord passing around the leg to be turned. As the treadle was depressed the leg revolved at speed as the lathe tools were used on it. The village turners of the Chiltern beechwoods normally supplied their output to the furniture factories of High Wycombe. The wood from hand-cleft logs was considered to be of a higher quality because the cleaving took place along the grain of the wood as opposed to the cross-grain cut frequently obtained with a saw.

13 Another pole lathe worker was George William ailey, the bowl turner of Buckleburry Common, erkshire, here finishing a bowl with a knife in the oorway of his wooden hut. In the nineteenth century wl turning had been practised casually as a by-mployment by several generations of the Lailey mily, who were chiefly publicans and small farmers.

George William, the last turner, practised the craft as a sole means of livelihood, selling his elm wood bowls to London stores as well as to the many visitors he received after being publicized by H. V. Morton, travelling *In search of England* (1927).

114 Bundling cut and trimmed brown basket withies in the Athelney area of Somerset. Over half the country's basket willow was grown in the withy beds along the banks of the rivers Parrett and Tone, being made up locally into baskets or wicker furniture. There was considerable concern in the 1930s over the increasing imports of willow and basketware into the country and the consequent undercutting of the prices of the home producers.

115 *Right* Basket makers using stripped withy rods in small factory on King's Sedge Moor, Somerset. Oil lamps provided an even and moderate temperature to prevent the willow from becoming brittle. Both workers are sitting on their 'planks' and the right hand one is working his basket on a lapboard. The two pieces of wood to the left of each worker are the blocks used to hold the sticks upright while making square bases.

116 *Right, below* Thatching ricks at Mile End Farm, near Theale, Berkshire in the late 1930s. The farm was owned by H. A. Benyon of Englefield House and the wagon is still lettered with the name of his father, J. H. Benyon, a Lord Lieutenant of the county. After corn had been reaped by the binder it had to be stacked and protected from the weather by thatching until it could be threshed. These ricks are supported by iron rick stands. Photograph by Eric Guy.

117 Re-thatching a cottage with long straw at Fownhope, Herefordshire in 1935. The wagon serves as both ladder base and straw container. Photograph by M. Wight.

118 *Right* Harvesting thatching reed with a long-handled scythe at Slapton, south Devon, late April 1939. The bundles of cut reed are transported in the flat bottomed boats to nearby fields to dry. The reed harvester is wearing protective knee pads and reinforced leather gaiters.

119 *Right, below* Dressing a course of Norfolk reed with the leggett. The needles are used to fix the horizontal hazel sway in place by threading them through the reed with a tarred cord. This thatcher photographed in July 1936 was R. W. Farman of North Walsham, Norfolk, whose family had a long tradition of reed thatching. A thatched roof of Norfolk reed might last 50 years or more before it required renewal, compared to the 10 or 20 years expected of long straw.

120 Outside the wheelwright's workshop at Fritton, Norfolk, 1939. The adze held by the wheelwright was primarily employed for removing surplus wood in the making of wheel felloes. The manufacture of new wagons, even by the large town works that had taken over from the local wheelwrights, had virtually ceased by this date. The majority of village wheelwrights now functioned as general carpenters and repair shops.

121 *Right* This wheelwright, with the less fortunate bottom sawyer below him in the saw pit, is still using the pit saw, the only method of cutting a tree trunk into useable lengths before the introduction of power-driven machinery. Arthur Goddin set up as village wheelwright and carpenter in Pontrilas, south Herefordshire in 1907 after his apprenticeship to George Sayce, wheelwright of Grosmont, Monmouthshire. Photograph by M. Wight in 1920.

122 Blacksmith and his assistant shoeing a draught horse. The shoes of a farm horse, working mainly on soft ground might last up to three months. As the horse was still the predominant form of agricultural power in the inter-war years, every village possessed a shoeing and general smith who also undertook the repair of horse-drawn implements.

123 The forge interior of W. & H. Parfoot, Fittleworth, Sussex in spring 1938. The smiths are engaged in making up horseshoes. Photograph by G. G Garland.

124 Mrs Salisbury, a glove-stitcher of Tibberton, Worcestershire in 1934. She is using the pedal-operate 'donkey' to hold the leather while stitching. Glove-making was a late surviving example of an industry employing outworkers, who undertook the making up of gloves from the washed, tanned, dyed and dressed sheepskin delivered to their homes. The most important centres of the industry at this time were Worcester, Yeovil and the west Oxfordshire towns of Woodstock, Charlbury and Chipping Norton. Photograph by M. Wight.

Transport

5 Harvest wagon passing through the north ...rkshire village of Long Wittenham. The wagon is the ...oduct of a local wheelwright employing the design ...ditionally found in the Vale of the White Horse. This example has spindle sides, a full bow curving down over the rear wheels and a deep waisted bed to allow for the turning of the fore-carriage into the body frame. Photograph by Eric Guy.

126 Team of three Hereford oxen on the Cirencester Park estate of Earl Bathurst with oxman Ted Smith. Horse teams brought loads of coal from the station to the gates of the estate where the oxen took over. As they were used only on the non-metalled estate roads it was not necessary to shoe them. They are working in modified horse harness with specially designed collars rather than the traditional wooden yokes with which oxen had been worked on the South Downs of Sussex until 1929. Photograph by M. Wight (see also Plate 6).

127 *Right* Bringing home branch trimmings for firewood near Andover, Hampshire. Farm and estate workers were often allowed to buy cheaply a cord of wood (nominally six feet by three feet by three feet of pieces not more than four inches in diameter). The vehicle is a flat-bodied trolley probably of local manufacture rather than a factory-built type. Photograph by Eric Guy.

128 *Below* Hauling a timber carriage on to the road in difficult conditions after heavy rain near Hildenborough, Kent, February 1931.

129 An International Harvester Titan tractor with two wagon-loads of grain near Dorking, Surrey about 1920. These are factory-built boat wagons. The adaptation of horse-drawn transport for tractor haulage was characteristic of the early period of tractor use in Britain. The Titan 10–20 tractor was manufactured by the International Harvester Company at their Milwaukee, Wisconsin plant from 1914 to the early 1920s. Despite its rather primitive design and appearance it proved remarkably successful, several thousands being sent to Britain in the later years of the First World War.

130 *Right* Moving a farm by train. In March 1939 Sir John Lloyd moved from Sevenoaks, Kent to Cirencester, Gloucestershire. The pedigree Jerseys are leaving the special train at Cirencester station for road transport to their new home at Waterton House.

131 *Right, below* Loading strawberry chip baskets into shelved railway vans at Swanwick station, Hampshire, June 1936. Swanwick was the centre of a strawberry growing area just east of Southampton which possessed about ten per cent of England's strawberry acreage. Both horse-drawn spring wagons and motor vehicles were used by growers or hired carters to transport their fruit to the railheads from which special trains were operated by the Southern Railway to all parts of Britain (other than Kent and the eastern counties which produced strawberry crops of their own).

132 *Left* Building a new section of arterial road through the countryside to replace a difficult stretch which had become dangerous through the increased amount of motor traffic. This new three-and-a-half mile section of the York–Malton road was under construction to avoid the village of Whitwell on the Hill near Malton in the North Riding of Yorkshire. Although a light railway has been constructed to assist the transport of materials, horse-drawn tip-carts have still been found useful in preparing the new road bed. The old road with its AA box may be seen on the right.

133 *Left, below* Work in progress on the Kingston Bypass, Surrey in February 1937 in a stretch of countryside that was rapidly becoming urbanized. Here the concrete carriageway is under construction, the cement being delivered by a steam lorry.

134 Outside the garage at Husbands' Bosworth, Leicestershire. The photograph was part of a collection amassed by the Council for the Preservation of Rural England (founded in 1926) to illustrate a campaign against ugly roadside features of the contemporary landscape. Here there is a clutter of advertising and direction signs, including several erected by the AA and RAC (note the patrolman of the latter organization). It was considered that the thatched building, adapted to meet the requirements of the new motor age, was bearing too heavy a burden of advertising material, 'the sign merchants having done their damnedest'.

135 (a) & (b) Two CPRE propaganda photographs illustrating the Light Car and Motor Cycle Garage at Theale, Berkshire with its full content of signs and their subsequent removal. The Bullnose Morris is carrying a spare can of Shell petrol affixed to the running board.

136 *Right* The 1920s saw the spread of 'rosary' cafés, 'beading' the main roads and providing increasing numbers of lorry-drivers and day-trippers with a pull-in for tea and refreshments. This shanty was photographed by the CPRE at Newton Poppleford on the Exeter–Lyme Regis road in Devon It was criticized for its 'scaly hide' enamel signs.

137 The first delivery of soft fruit by air in Great Britain in June 1938. 1,200 lbs of freshly picked strawberries, grown by A. J. Varney of Cheddar, Somerset, were delivered by road to Weston Super Mare airport and loaded on to a D.H. Dragon aircraft of Western Airways. The plane landed at Birmingham Aerodrome 45 minutes later.

People

8 Lady Curre of Ifton Court, Chepstow,
nmouthshire. She was well-known for her prize-
winning Shorthorn herd, and also kept Kerry sheep and
Middle White pigs. Taken in March 1935.

9 *Left, above* Members of the South-Eastern Jersey
1b at a field meeting to inspect the herd of Brigadier-
neral F. C. More-Molyneaux of Loseley Park,
ildford, Surrey, August 1934.

) *Left* Pig-farmer, Mr Stephen Player of Whatton-in-
Vale, Nottinghamshire. With only a small herd of
sows and 2 boars – all pedigree Berkshires – Mr
yer achieved considerable success at the Royal
ithfield and other shows in 1936. Berkshires had
ained a reputation for low prolificacy and slow
turity but Player believed that these shortcomings
e caused more by poor management than by any
1 defect in the breed.

141 Meeting of the Guernsey club. Walter Dunkels,
owner of the Fernhill herd, invited members to inspect
his animals at Fernhill Park, Cranbourne, Berkshire, in
May 1935. Herd societies played an important part in
improving livestock, especially before the Government
introduced the Accredited Herd Scheme in 1935 – to
upgrade standards and to free herds from tuberculosis.
Even then breeders were initially opposed to the
Government measure, on the grounds that it only
introduced another grade of milk and did not provide
compensation for killing infected animals.

142 A Somerset farmer: Mr E. F. Case of Withycombe Farm, Washford, near Taunton, Somerset. Taken in January 1939 (see also Plate 49).

143 *Below* At Congleton Cattle Market, Cheshire, 1939.

144 *Right* Gypsy encampment. The caravan appears to be a 'modern' open-lot van – a simplified form of construction, established as a type in the 1930s. A Dorothy Hartley photograph.

145 Gypsy camp at Malvern Link, Worcestershire, 1939. A Miss Wight photograph.

146 Washing with a dolly and tub outside Benfield Farmhouse, Bredwardine, Herefordshire, 1936.

147 At the village pump. It is interesting to note that the countrywoman shown here is wearing a sun-bonnet. This distinctly English form of rural headgear replaced the small cap, with a straw hat worn over it for out-of-doors use, during the first half of the nineteenth century. Typically, the sunbonnet had a stiffened brim, lines of ruching and cording across the crown and a frill or curtain over the neck and shoulders. It was chiefly worn to avoid sunburn, but also gave good protection against wind and, to some extent, rain. Sunbonnets continued to be worn during this period, especially for field-work such as hoeing, stooking corn and gleaning, or hop and fruit picking. However, they became increasingly 'old-fashioned' and their use gradually died out.

148 A dairy in Wensleydale, North Riding of Yorkshire, about 1934. A Dorothy Hartley photograph.

149 *Below* A knife-grinder at Winchcombe, Gloucestershire in 1936. By this time the tinker – once a familiar figure in the villages – was only infrequently seen. The low cost of the equipment, however, meant that it could be afforded by those with little capital and provided men who could find no other work with the means to earn a modest living. Some, indeed, enjoyed the freedom of the itinerant's life and preferred it to more regular employment. A Miss Wight photograph.

150 *Right* Feeding farmyard cats, *c.* 1940. Photograph by Eric Guy.

151 *Right, below* Taking the team home. The horseman carries a basket in one hand and keeps a relaxed but firm grip on the hame rein (near the bit) with the other. Horses require a rest and a feed when away from the stable for more than 4–$4\frac{1}{2}$ hours, and the nosebags hung on the hames of the horse on the left probably contained a mixture of oats and chaff. Note, too, the use of ear-caps or muffs, with tassels, to keep the flies away. These muffs are of a common design supplied by firms specializing in horse clothing, although such humble items were often made by the horseman's wife. Photograph by Eric Guy.

152 Keeping a pig was a traditional means of supplementing the rural worker's earnings, while also ensuring a supply of tasty meals for the family. The photograph shows Mr Moody, of Downton Pig Club, and his wife. This Wiltshire pig club was started in 1910, and was reported in the *Farmer and Stock-Breeder* almost 30 years later as being a model enterprise such as the Small Pig-Keepers' Council would wish to see thriving throughout the country. Members included carpenters, lorry drivers, plumbers and gardeners. They bought weaners from pedigree breeders, kept them in sheds at the bottom of their gardens, fed them on garden scraps and returned their manure to the soi They reckoned that a pig would weigh some nine or te score pounds by nine months and that the profit taker was equivalent to one pig in three.

Village Life

153 Bread dole, Aymestrey, North Herefordshire. During the Middle Ages, wealthy people often left money in their wills to the church-wardens of the parish to provide an annual gift of bread, cheese or cakes to the poor. By the twentieth century Church doles were often purely customary, being distributed, without condition, to those parishioners who asked for them. The photographer was Miss Wight and although she records that the day was Good Friday, the print is otherwise undated. Probably 1930s.

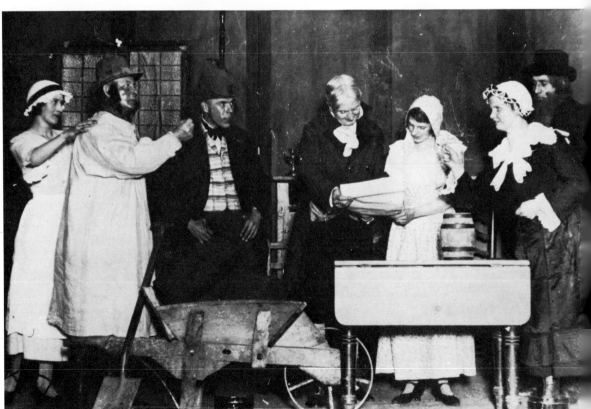

154 Pace-egg play, Midgley, West Riding of Yorkshire, 1935. The collecting of eggs from house to house by 'Jolly-boys' took place at Easter and was widespread in the north of England. Not all pace-egging included a play, which, if present, was of the 'hero-combat' or 'St George' type. The play at Midgley is known to have been performed until 1914 and was revived by the local headmaster in 1935; the text being conflated from other sources and additional fanciful characters introduced. The flowered headpiece with strings of beads, in place of the more usual paper strips or ribbons concealing the face, are interesting; the rest of the costume is vestigial.

155 *Left* Village drama, Castle Cary, Somerset. This play, 'Conjurer Lantern', was written by John Read, who founded the Camel Play Actors in 1910 to perform his own plays written in the dialect of his native Somerset. He hoped to inspire a revival of dialect in England, similar to that initiated by Cecil Sharp in folk song and dance. The photograph was taken in 1934.

156 Nether Stowey Women's Friendly Society annual club walk, Somerset. After a church service, members walked in procession around the village, preceded by the Society's banner and a band. On this occasion six children carrying baskets of flowers were also included. Afterwards there would almost certainly have been a lunchtime feast with a fair or fête in the afternoon. This photograph was taken sometime during the 1920s.

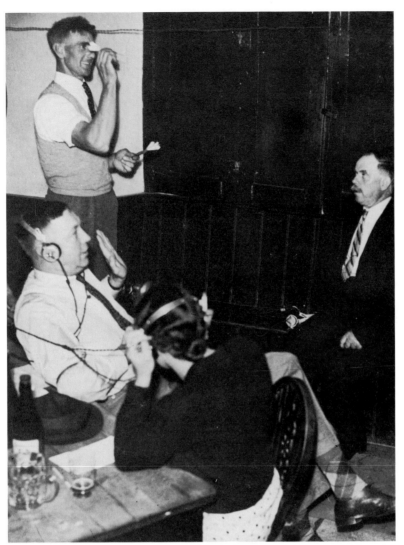

157 Broadcasting a darts match, June 1939. The match was between Wiltshire, represented by The Black Horse, Teffont Magna, and Somerset, represented by the Crown Hotel, Burnham-on-Sea. The Somerset team was recorded by Ben Travers of Rookery Nook fame and the Wiltshire team by the well-known farming journalist and writer, A. G. Street. The photograph shows Arthur Street, seated with headphones: the thrower was Jimmy Yates. Wiltshire were beaten in a match of 501, when they still had 114 to get.

Recreation

158 Judging at the Golden Retriever Club Sanction Show at Herons' Buckhold, near Pangbourne, Berkshire, June 1934. The best dog and winner of the Patiala Cup was Anningsley Fox, seen on the right of the photograph. He is held by his owner Mr H. Venables Kyrke; also shown are Mrs Kyrke (third from right), Lady Ursula Abbey (far left, seated) and the Hon. Lady Ward (second from left, standing). Photograph by Eric Guy.

159 *Left* The South Berkshire
hounds passing a plough team while
running at Ufton, Berkshire.
Photograph by Eric Guy, probably
late 1930s.

161 Otter hounds meet, Tarrington, Herefordshire, 1939. Otter-hunting
declined in Edwardian times, although it still retained its popularity in some
areas. No longer was the animal harpooned in mid-stream; instead sportsmen
stood in line across the river in an attempt to 'tail' the otter, that is to catch
it by the 'rudder'. Hounds, too, were employed in greater numbers. The
season lasted from Shrovetide until the autumn. Photograph by Miss Wight.

160 *Left* The opening of the grouse
shooting season. Lord Swinton's
shoot on Pott Moor, Masham,
Yorkshire, August 1937. The
photograph shows the panniers
being loaded with the bag at the wall
butts.

THE FOLEY ARMS HOTEL.

162 *Left* Champion school sports team, in the small village of Stanford-le-Hope, on the Essex marshes, 1931. The Essex County Shield (shown centre of photograph) was awarded for proficiency in sport and education; winning this shield, together with the cricket and football cups, was an outstanding achievement for a village school.

163 Village cricket match, probably 1930s.

164 Maeshafn Youth Hostel, Merseyside. In the late nineteenth and early twentieth centuries, numerous organizations were set up to provide young working men and women from the industrial areas with cheap country holidays. But Youth Hostels as such were started in Germany by a school teacher, Richard Schirrman, after 1910 and spread to France and Holland in the 1920s. The British Youth Hostel Association was established in 1930 and by the outbreak of war had a national membership of 83,000, with 224 hostels open in different parts of the country.

165 Bathing while on a caravan holiday. Horse caravanning for pleasure can be traced back to the 1880s, although its popularity declined with the coming of the motor car and the change in road surfaces and traffic conditions in the 1920s. It was always an expensive form of recreation. In 1923, when this photograph was taken, the cost of renting of a van might be anything from two to three guineas a week; the horse might cost as much as £4 and his feed amount to 20 shillings a week. The motor trailer caravan avoided the problem of horse management, but it was not until car ownership increased greatly in the 1930s that there was a surge of interest in motor caravan holidays.

Social Issues

166 Unemployed men from distressed areas being taught farm work. There were numerous attempts during the depression years to resettle urban families on the land or to assist their emigration overseas. The Land Settlement Association took a leading part in this work, although this photograph illustrates the contribution of the Salvation Army. Its training colony at Hadleigh in Essex, set up in the late 19th century, provided instruction in a range of agricultural skills. The farm apprentices shown here were afterwards to find jobs in Australia; a country eager to encourage British settlers at this time. Taken in March 1938.

167 *Left* Young farmers. The Wallingford Farm
Training Colony, at Turner's Court, Berkshire, was
established to train boys who would 'otherwise be
unemployed and unemployable' for skilled work on the
land. The farm comprised nearly 1,000 acres on the
western end of the Chilterns, where 300 boys between
14 and 17 years of age – many of them orphans –
received a complete course in agriculture. The stock on
the farm included three herds of Ayrshire cattle, about
800 Large White pigs, 3,500 head of poultry and 21
horses. The colony was self-supporting and any surplus
produce was sold.

168 *Left, below* Agricultural trade unionism. The
photograph shows George Edwards, founder of the
National Union of Agricultural Workers (holding the
fork, centre). The location is south Norfolk and the
occasion most likely to have been one of the three
elections fought in that division between 1918 and
1923. Edwards was returned as a Labour MP in the
1920 by-election – the second time that a former
agricultural labourer had won a Norfolk constituency;
Joseph Arch having previously represented north-
west Norfolk in the late nineteenth century.

169 Tithe protests. The 1930s saw a revival of farmers'
resistance to paying tithes. In the Middle Ages one
tenth of the annual produce of each parish was allowed
by law for the support of the clergy: a payment
commuted in 1836 to a smaller rent-charge. But the
fact that agriculture was the only industry taxed to
help maintain the church was bitterly resented, and in
the early thirties many farmers – already threatened by
bankruptcy – refused to pay. Thousands of court orders
were issued, and attempts by auctioneers to sell
farmers' goods often led to pitched battles with the
authorities.

This photograph shows protestors carrying an effigy
of the Archbishop of Canterbury (which was later to be
burned at the stake) during an unsuccessful sale of nine
dairy cows seized for arrears of tithes at Beechbrook
Farm, Westwell, near Ashford, Kent, April 1935. On
the right of the picture, wearing spectacles, is Mr R. M.
Kedward, the owner of the farm and a leading
spokesman for the National Tithe Payers Association.
Queen Anne features on the placard because during her
reign tithes became part of the Church's revenue known
as Queen Anne's Bounty.

170 The 1936 Tithe Act was a vain attempt to settle
the issue. The Government paid the Church £53 million
compensation for the abolition of tithes, but sought to
recover the money from farmers over a 60-year period.
Each farmer was to pay less than before but, if he
defaulted, the amount – instead of being recoverable
from goods – could be recovered directly from the
farmer's bank account; a quieter but more effective
approach.

The photograph records the great protest meeting
organized against the proposed legislation in June
1936. Three thousand farmers and their wives formed a
mile long procession from the Embankment, ending in
a mass-rally in Hyde Park, where they were addressed
by Lady Eve Balfour and Sir Stafford Cripps. Most of
the farmers wore straw plaits in buttonholes and many
carried scythes, hoes, spades or forks. This was the
largest single demonstration, although a vigorous
campaign against tithes was continued until the
outbreak of war.

171 Mr E. R. Whitehouse, National Conservative
candidate for Northern Cornwall, helping with the
milking on a farm near Launceston, November 1935.
The mood of the country before the General Election
held in that month was reported to be apathetic; the
Farmers' Weekly noting that, despite events in Europe,
'The great feature in many constituencies was the
difficulty of securing audiences for political meetings'.
The National Government under Stanley Baldwin was
returned with an increased majority – about 250.

The Coming of War

172 In the summer of 1939 British agriculture was once again faced with the challenge of having to produce enough to feed the nation in the event of war. Here King George VI, Queen Elizabeth and Queen Mary are reviewing some 20,000 National Service volunteers in Hyde Park: passing the saluting base are members of the Women's Land Service Corps – soon to be reconstituted as the Women's Land Army. Taken in July 1939.

173 Children with gas-masks over their shoulders watching threshing at Westerham, Kent, September 1939. The steam traction-engine shown here was made by the local firm of Aveling and Porter, of Rochester.

74 *Left* The Minister of Agriculture, Sir Reginald Dorman-Smith (with pipe) at Southampton to view the town's 'Grow More Food' activities. The day was also notable for Southampton Allotments Association's 25th anniversary. Dorman-Smith was a former President of the National Farmers' Union; he was appointed in December 1935 following his victory as a National Conservative candidate at Petersfield in the General Election. Sir John Reith, who accompanied the Minister, is seen on the right of the photograph. Taken May 1940.

75 Hop-pickers in Kent digging trenches to be used as shelters in case of air raids. Thousands of men and women from the East End of London continued to spend their annual 'holiday' in the hop fields – earning a small extra income and a much needed respite from London's bombing. Taken August 1940.

176 Harvest of Nazi planes:
Messerschmitt 109 shot down in a
field of oats in Wiltshire, August
1940.